THE ROAD BEST TRAVELED

RAY PRITCHARD

CROSSWAY BOOKS • WHEATON, ILLINOIS
A DIVISION OF GOOD NEWS PUBLISHERS

The Road Best Traveled

Copyright © 1995 by Ray Pritchard

Published by Crossway Books
      a division of Good News Publishers
      1300 Crescent Street
      Wheaton, Illinois 60187

Cover photo: Carlos Navajas

Printed in the United States of America

ISBN 0-89107-851-7

For Marlene,
my wife and my best friend.
God speaks to me through her.

Table of Contents

Acknowledgments

Many people had a hand in making this book a reality. My special thanks to: Brian Ondracek, who saw the potential before anyone else; Ted Griffin, whose expert editing made this a better book; Marti Alt, Ann Baer, Brian Bill, Rich and Pam Griffin, Kurt and Liz Johnson, and Mildred Stratton, all of whom read an early draft and offered many helpful suggestions; my Promise Keepers group, for their prayers and encouragement; the elders of Calvary Memorial Church, who gave me the time to complete the project; Marlene, who cheerfully carried an extra load at home; my three sons Josh, Mark, and Nick, because I promised I would mention their names somewhere in the book.

Introduction

This is a book I never intended to write. I say that because it is based on a series of sermons I never intended to preach. It happened like this. Early one January I laid out my preaching plans for the year, and they didn't include preaching on God's will. But that began to change somewhere along the way, perhaps about March or April. Almost every day I found myself talking with people who sought advice about major decisions they were facing. A job change . . . a move across the country . . . where to go to college . . . a possible call to foreign missions . . . hiring new employees . . . buying a new home . . . marriage, divorce, or remarriage . . . whether or not to have more children.

Then there were the hard questions. "Why did my father get cancer?" "How can I be 100 percent certain of God's will?" "Does God speak to us through dreams and visions today?" "Is it wrong to go to R-rated movies?" "Should I put out a fleece?" The list seemed to have no end.

One day in July I began jotting notes on the will of God. Out flowed ideas, quotes, comments made to me over the years, stories of people searching for direction, crucial Scriptures, pressing questions, areas of common confusion, and popular misunderstandings. On and on I wrote, page after page, surprising myself by the sheer volume I generated in only two hours.

But I still didn't have a sermon series. How would I take that mass of uncongealed study and bring order from the chaos? I left the matter alone for a week or so, coming back to it during my vacation in August. We spent the first few days on a lake in southern Michigan. Then we traveled north to the Upper Peninsula, to Sault Sainte Marie, and west to Wisconsin where we spent one rainy night in Green Bay. I wrote notes as we traveled, pulling my scattered thoughts together as we motored through one small town after another. We arrived back in Oak Park for one day, washed our clothes, and set out for the Illinois State Fair in Springfield. Several days later we pushed farther south to visit my younger brother in Mississippi, who graciously allowed us the free run of his camp. While the boys went swimming in the lake, I jotted down more notes. Next we traveled to Alabama to visit my older brother, then turned north to make our way back to Chicago. More notes, thoughts, and ideas flowed from my pen onto paper as we made our way through bluegrass country into Indiana.

By the time we got home, the series had come together in my mind. Several weeks later I preached the first sermon: "Does God Still Guide?" The response was so encouraging that I knew this was what God had wanted all along. True preaching is always a two-way conversation between the pulpit and the pew. The preacher listens, then speaks, then listens again.

What you are about to read is more than the sermons I preached. During the year since I finished that series, I have continued to listen to the voices of many people as they told me about their journeys with the Lord. Several brand-new chapters have been added. But I thought you ought to know the background because this book was born out of the real-life questions of people standing at various crossroads of life. There is nothing theoretical in the following pages. Everything here was forged on the anvil of human experience.

That's why this book is filled with stories. Some of them have happy endings; some don't. Many of them tell about decisions made, but the final result is not yet known.

As you read this book, please take time to consider the questions at the end of each chapter. Don't skip them. They are designed to help you grapple with the major concepts and then to apply them to your own life.

After writing this book, I am more convinced than ever that you *can* discover God's will for your life. More than that, I am fully persuaded that *if you want to do God's will, you will do it.* If that sounds exciting, turn the page and let's get started.

CHAPTER ONE

Does God Still Guide?

The year was 1915, and America was inching toward World War I. In Liverpool, England, a young man decided to return to New Hampshire while he still had the chance. As he prepared to leave England, he composed a poem that he later insisted had been simply a gentle joke written for a good friend. Yet that composition became one of the best-loved poems of the twentieth century.

Two roads diverged in a yellow wood,
And sorry I could not travel both
And be one traveler, long I stood
And looked down one as far as I could
To where it bent in the undergrowth;

Then took the other, just as fair,
And having perhaps the better claim,
Because it was grassy and wanted wear;
Though as for that the passing there
Had worn them really about the same,

And both that morning equally lay
In leaves no step had trodden black.
Oh, I kept the first for another day!
Yet knowing how way leads on to way,
I doubted if I should ever come back.

I shall be telling this with a sigh
Somewhere ages and ages hence:
Two roads diverged in a wood, and I—
I took the one less traveled by,
And that has made all the difference.

The poet was Robert Frost. His poem is known around the world as "The Road Not Taken." All of us have been there!

We have all come to the crossroads of life where two roads diverged, one winding off to the left, the other disappearing in the distance to the right. We stood at the fork in the road and wondered, Should I go this way or should I go that way?

OUR DECISIONS MAKE US

Our decisions really do matter. *We make our decisions, and our decisions turn around and make us.* We face so many questions:

- Should I get married? If the answer is yes, should I marry Joe or Jake? Should I marry Susan or Sally?

- Should I go to college? If the answer is yes, should I go to Alabama or Penn State or UCLA?

- I've been offered a new job. It's a good one. But I already have a good job. Should I take the new position? Or should I hold on to what I have?

- We have two children. We're thinking about having a third. Should we have another one? Should we think about adopting?

- Is God calling me to the mission field? How can I be sure? Three mission boards are interested in me. How do I know which one to choose?

YOU CAN'T GO BACK

We make our decisions, and our decisions turn around and make us. If you go to UCLA, you won't go to Alabama or Penn State or anywhere else—at least not this year. Even if you think you might transfer next year, that won't be the same as going there this year. And if you marry Sue instead of Barbara, that one decision will stay with you—for better or for worse—for the rest of your life. Even if for some reason you get a divorce that ends your marriage, you'll live with the consequences forever. You can major in biology or business administration—you can even take a double major if you like; but whichever path you take, you can't go back and be an eighteen-year-old college freshman again.

Sometimes the slightest decisions, made in haste and without much thought, turn out to have the greatest impact. Years ago while pastoring a church in the Los Angeles area, a letter arrived one day asking if I would consider moving to Texas to become the first pastor of a new church in a Dallas suburb. I had never heard of the church or the man who signed the letter. That particular day I was not in the mood to consider moving anywhere. Nothing in the letter sounded particularly inviting or intriguing. In fact, I couldn't think of a single reason to get excited about moving back to Texas. But what to do about the invitation? I had to respond one way or the other. As I stood by my desk thinking about it, the envelope in my hand, I tried to decide whether to throw it away or toss it on my desk. For some reason that I still don't fully understand, I tossed the envelope on my desk.

From that rather haphazard, spur-of-the-moment decision came a major redirection of my life. One thing led to another, and I ended up as a pastor for five and a half very eventful years in Garland, Texas. I didn't see it then, and I couldn't have known how important that casual decision was. I'm sure I didn't pray about whether to toss the envelope in the trash or on my desk. Looking back on it, I had no sense that I was standing at a crossroads. Two roads diverged in a yellow wood that afternoon in California, and by choosing not to throw away an unexpected letter, I unknowingly chose "the road less traveled."

THE "ROMANCE" OF GOD'S WILL

Most of us have similar stories. Just as a massive ship is guided by a tiny rudder, our lives often turn on small decisions and unexpected events. An unplanned phone call, a "chance" conversation in the hallway, a friend we "happen" to meet in a restaurant, a fragment of a remembered dream, a book we meant to return but didn't, the dry cleaning we forgot to pick up, a newspaper story that led to an idea that became a dissertation topic that earned a degree that opened a door to a job in another country. It happens all the time.

Life *is* unpredictable. That's the romance of trying to discover God's will for your life. Does the word "romance" sound unusual to you in connection with God's will? It shouldn't. As we move on together through the chapters of this book, we'll discover that *knowing God's will is really all about knowing God*. But knowing God can never be reduced to a mechanical formula, any more than the marriage between a man and a woman can be reduced to Three Steps or Four Keys or Five Rules. Since knowing God is central to knowing His will, what you will find are biblical stories that, like pieces of a puzzle, fit together to give us a better understanding of what it means to know God personally. Out of those stories we will draw principles that show us how God's will is discovered in the outworking of the ordinary affairs of life.

MORE THAN A BIRTHDAY CAKE

I can't say that I've always looked at God's will this way. Years ago I looked at the subject in a rather mechanical fashion—"Do these three things and you'll discover God's will." Unfortunately, the only thing I discovered was that the "three things" don't always work as advertised. The "three things" are indeed helpful, and even essential, just as remembering your spouse's birthday is essential to a healthy marriage. But marriage is more than a birthday cake, and knowing God's will is more than having a quiet time in the morning.

What, then, is this book all about? I propose to share the theme of this book in one sentence. If you want to know what *The Road Best Traveled* is all about, here it is: *God wants you to know His will more than you want to know it, and therefore He takes personal responsibility to see that you discover it.* Knowing God's will is ultimately God's problem, not yours. The sooner you realize that, the happier you will be. Too many people agonize over God's will as if God were playing a cosmic game of hide and seek. The entire Bible teaches us the opposite, that our God seeks us. He continually takes the initiative to reveal Himself to us. Therefore, knowing God's will is simply a subsection of the larger question of knowing God personally.

That's the whole book in a nutshell. If you're looking for a quick-fix approach, this is probably not the book for you. But if you would like to know God better, *and through knowing God learn more about knowing His will*, read on.

WHAT THIS BOOK CAN'T DO

One disclaimer: if you are currently in the yellow wood standing at the crossroads as you read these words, and if you are hoping that this book will tell you which road to take, you will probably be disappointed. Nothing in these pages will make your decisions for you. You'll still have to choose between UCLA and Florida State or between moving to South Carolina or staying in Oregon. If you're wondering whether to marry Joe or Harry, you'll have to decide that for yourself. No book written by mortal man can make your choices for you.

As you move through these chapters, I can promise you some new insights into who God is and how He reveals Himself to His children. I'm sure that you'll approach your decisions with more confidence and less fear once you discover how much God wants you to know His will. Nothing is more comforting to the child of God than knowing that amid the confusion of everyday life God is slowly leading you along the path of His will. In fact, He is working in and through your decisions (and often in spite of your decisions) to see that His will is actually done in your life.

A PERSONAL WORD

I have a personal interest in this subject because I have agonized over the will of God. Recently I took a look back over the forty-two years of my life. *I realized that who I am today is the result of all the decisions I have made until now.* I am the result of hundreds and thousands of decisions, many of which did not seem very important at the time. I have already mentioned tossing the envelope from Texas on my desk instead of in the trash can. But there were many others.

- When I was in the fourth grade my friend Tommy Thompson joined the band. I joined soon after he did, learned how to play the trombone, and saved up money to go to the Cotton Carnival in Memphis, Tennessee, when I was about thirteen years old. There I visited a radio station and met a disc jockey who showed me the news as it came off the AP wire. When he gave me a handful of yellow sheets with news reports on them, I was so excited I could hardly sleep that night.

- When I was in the seventh grade I began stopping by Ira's Gift and Book Shop. Every week Ira Schnell gave me a copy of a Christian magazine. It was the first place I ever saw the Gospel of Jesus Christ clearly set forth in print.

- When I was a senior in high school, I decided to enter the Junior Civitan Public Speaking Competition, won the local contest, and went on to the regional competition.

- When I graduated from high school I was offered a college scholarship, and without much thought I said no because it wasn't the right place for me.

- Three years later I took a deep breath and said hi to that cute girl who was the secretary of the music department in the college that I attended.

- The year after my father died, and my faith had taken a major hit, I chose—almost by throwing a dart at a piece of paper—to go to Paraguay for a summer missions trip that turned my life and our marriage completely around.

From one decision came a love of music and journalism; from another the realization that yes, I could stand and speak well before an audience; from yet another a courtship that led to marriage; from another a major moment of personal renewal.

Over the years I have made thousands of decisions, many of which seemed trivial at the time. But taken together they have made me exactly who I am today. The same is true for all of us. *You make your decisions, and then your decisions turn around and make you.*

THE CRUCIAL QUESTION

There are many different ways to ask this question. You could ask: how can I, a mere mortal, ever discover what Almighty God wants me to do? Or you might wonder, how can I bring God into the reality of my daily life? Or you could go right to the bottom line: where is God when I have to make a really tough decision?

Or you could ask it this way: does God still guide? In the moments of life when you have to make a tough decision, when you are in the woods with the two roads diverging in front of you, can you count on God to help you?

Some years ago when I was in a desperate moment of my own life, I stumbled across Psalm 48:14, "For this God is our God for ever and ever; he will be our guide even to the end." I had lost my job and had no prospects on the horizon. I had a wife, three children, and a mortgage payment to make. When I desperately needed to know what God wanted me to do, this verse was precious to me. It sustained me in some dark moments when I wondered if I would be able to take care of my family. Out of that crucible I discovered that God does indeed guide His children.

FOLLOW THAT CLOUD!

There are many stories in the Bible that illustrate this truth. But few episodes grip the imagination like the story of the cloud and the pillar of fire that led God's people through the wilderness.

The nation of Israel was leaving the land of Egypt. After they crossed the Red Sea, they would go to Mount Sinai, and eventually they would come to the Promised Land. In the process of leaving the safety and security of Egypt, something amazing happened. Exodus 13:20-22 tells the story:

> After leaving Succoth they camped at Etham on the edge of the desert. By day the Lord went ahead of them in a pillar of cloud to guide them on their way and by night in a pillar of fire to give them light, so that they could travel by day or night. Neither the pillar of cloud by day nor the pillar of fire by night left its place in front of the people.

The desert was behind them, the Red Sea was in front of them, and the Egyptians were closing fast from the rear. Unable to go back to Egypt, trapped between water in front of them and the armies of Pharaoh to the rear, the people of God found themselves between the devil and the deep blue sea, you might say. Even if they somehow made it across the vast stretch of water, they faced an unknown future. As bad as Pharaoh had been, at least in Egypt they felt secure—they knew what to expect. But what would they do now that they were leaving their security behind them?

God answered their concern by sending them a moving pillar to guide them on their way. During the day the pillar was a visible cloud in the sky. During the night the cloud became a blazing pillar of fire. That provided visible, unmistakable guidance twenty-four hours a day, seven days a week. All they had to do was follow the cloud and the fire and they would be safe.

Numbers 9:15-23 explains how the pillar of fire actually worked. The passage is a bit long, but I find it fascinating in its details:

> On the day the tabernacle, the Tent of the Testimony, was set up, the cloud covered it. From evening till morning the cloud above the tabernacle looked like fire. That is how it continued to be; the cloud covered it, and at night it looked like fire. Whenever the cloud lifted from above the Tent, the Israelites set out; wherever the cloud settled, the Israelites camped. At the LORD's command the Israelites set out, and at his command they encamped. As long as the cloud stayed over the tabernacle, they remained in camp. When the cloud remained over the tabernacle a long time, the Israelites obeyed the LORD's order and did not set out. Sometimes the cloud was over the tabernacle only a few days; at the LORD's command they would encamp, and then at his command they would set out. Sometimes the cloud stayed only from evening till morning, and when it lifted in the morning, they set out. Whether by day or by night, whenever the cloud lifted, they set out. Whether the cloud stayed over the tabernacle for two days or a month or a year, the Israelites would remain in camp and not set out; but when it lifted, they would set out. At the LORD's command they encamped, and at the LORD's command they set out. They obeyed the LORD's order, in accordance with his command through Moses.

Using this story as a guide, I want to share with you four lessons from the cloud and the fire that explain to us something about how God guides His people.

LESSON #1:
God's guidance is revealed to us one step at a time

Numbers 9 makes this very clear. The cloud would lift, and they would go. As long as the cloud kept moving, they would follow. When it stopped, they would stop. Sometimes it would stop for a night and go the next morning. Then it would stop for a few days, and they would stop for a few days. The Israelites never knew from moment to moment or day to day what the cloud was going to do next.

Many Christians trip over this very point because they want to see ten steps ahead before they will take the first step. But life doesn't work that way. God rarely shows you ten steps in advance. He normally leads you one step at a time. He will lead you a step, then He'll lead you another step, and then He'll lead you another step. After He's led you ten steps, you look back and say, "How did I get from there to here?" Then you realize it was just step by step by step.

LESSON #2:
God's guidance demands our obedience
whether it makes sense to us or not

One day the cloud would just stop in the middle of the desert; so that's where the people of Israel set up camp. Ten days later, it would suddenly begin to move again. Why? Why not ten weeks? Or ten months? Or why not just keep moving? No one—not even Moses—knew the answers to those questions. Many days it didn't make any sense at all.

God's guidance is often like that. *Sometimes God keeps you moving when you would rather stop.* That's happening to one of my close friends as I write these words. All his life he has lived in the Chicago area. His life is here, his children are happy here, his wife is from this area, he knows and understands Chicago. Several years ago he started a new job with a national firm headquartered in a major southern city. For a year he flew in and out of Chicago, visiting customers from coast to coast. As a reward for his good work, his new company offered to make him president of a brand-new division. There was only one condition: he had to move to the home office. For months he agonized, prayed, sought godly counsel, waited for God to open other doors. At the same time he became an elder at our church, and he and his wife became leaders in our contemporary worship service. More than once I have heard him say, "I have no idea why God is doing this because I'd rather stay in Chicago." But in spite of all that, he is moving to a new state and entering a new culture, because for him and his family the cloud is moving on.

KEEP YOUR BAGS PACKED

Can you imagine what it was like to wander in the wilderness for forty years? You are in year twenty-three—only seventeen more years to go! For the last fourteen years it seems like you've been moving in circles in the desert. Finally the cloud stops. You're somewhere south of Kadesh-Barnea, about a hundred miles from Zoar, twenty-seven miles from Hazeroth, and roughly three miles from the end of the world. They call this place the "Desert of Zin." It's hot, rocky, barren, dusty—not a sign of life for miles in any direction. But the cloud has finally stopped. So you start to set up camp. You get the tent up and find some rocks to make a temporary sheepfold. You think to yourself, "Well, it looks like we're going to be here for a while." There's an oasis just over the next hill where you can get water. The next morning the cloud lifts. That makes you angry; so you look at the sky and have a conversation with the Lord: "What's going on? We just arrived. I just fed the sheep. I just put up the tent. What are You doing?" And the Lord says, "What I'm doing is moving. If you are going to follow Me, you are going to have to move with Me."

"LORD, WE'VE BEEN HERE LONG ENOUGH"

The other side is also true. *Sometimes the Lord says, "Stay" when we would rather be moving.* A friend wrote recently to say that she is struggling over this very point. Now that she and her husband have retired, they have plenty of time on their hands. Both of them would love to use their gifts in the Lord's work. But no opportunities have presented themselves. My friend wrote of "times when God puts you (the empty vessel) back in the cupboard, clean, but doesn't use you to cook His soup. I know that our part is just to be there—ready for His use, but it's boring." Then she added these perceptive words: "Shame on me for saying I am bored with my Christian life. But—this restlessness, yet not being able to change anything—is hard!" She and her husband are ready to move on. Why is the cloud standing still?

I don't know the answer to that. All I know is this: sometimes God says, "Wait" when we would rather move. Chuck Swindoll calls waiting the hardest discipline in the Christian life. I agree. That is why the psalmist says, "Be still before the LORD and wait patiently for him" (Psalm 37:7).

Let this lesson soak into your soul: *God's guidance demands our obedience, even when it makes no sense to us.* Sometimes God moves when we want to stay. Sometimes God says, "Stay" when we would rather move on and get our life going again.

LESSON #3:
God's guidance changes its character according to the need of the moment

During the day when the Israelites needed to see a cloud, God provided a cloud; but at night when the cloud would be invisible, the cloud looked like fire. God had one way of showing Himself to them during the day and another way of showing Himself at night.

That leads me to this conclusion: *God's guidance is always there, but His means of guiding us change from moment to moment.* Consider the implications of that statement. God is not obligated to lead you in the same way He leads somebody else. God is not obligated to deal with you today in the same way He dealt with you yesterday or the way He is going to deal with you tomorrow.

WHICH HOUSE SHOULD WE BUY?

That's an important principle to learn because so many of us have a very narrow view of God. We think that since God dealt with our best friend a certain way, He's therefore obligated to deal with us in the same way. "Lord, You answered her prayer that way. Now please do the same for me." God says, "No deal."

I've always admired (and perhaps slightly envied) those people who seem to have a direct connection with the Lord. When the time comes to make a major decision, they always seem to have an unusual experience, a startling answer to prayer, or an unexplainable "coincidence" that happens to them at just the right moment. In fact, some of my friends routinely expect such things to happen to them so that—from the outside at least—decision-making seems to come easily to them.

Not so with me. I've discovered over the years that I tend to agonize over big decisions. Sometimes the moment comes when you just have to make up your mind. As I write these words, my family is in the midst of moving from one house to another. To be more specific, we've already sold our home and as of this moment don't know where we are going next. This happened because our home sold too fast—in eight days to be exact. The people who are buying our home made us an offer we couldn't refuse, but they also want to take possession in about five weeks. So for the last few days, we've been scrambling, hastily visiting every other available home in Oak Park, Illinois, in our price range. I can summarize what we've found very simply: nice houses but too expensive; nice houses but too far from where we want to live; nice houses but too small; or nice houses that need lots of work. (It's not hard for me to determine God's will regarding that last category since I'm not a handyman.) But we did find a handful of houses that met our criteria. In fact, the day before yesterday we settled on two houses.

Both are within our price range, and both could potentially meet our needs. One is a charming, eighty-year-old, three-story home. It's very typical of the homes in Oak Park. It offers lots of room and lots of possibilities for the future. The other is a much newer, ranch-style home in a very nice section of central Oak Park. How does one make a decision when both houses are appealing and good arguments could be made for either one? It is small comfort to say that you can't go wrong either way (which is true). We have to choose one or the other. Or we have to find another house and start the process all over again.

Yesterday as I walked from the church down to the real

estate office to sign some papers, the thought hit me that no matter how much we discuss the matter or how many family discussions we have, there will always be some degree of uncertainty about our decision. In times past God has intervened to show us precisely what He wanted us to do. This time we are left to use our best judgment after spending time in prayer and in the Word and consulting many advisers (who tell us many different things).

MANY WAYS, ONE VOICE

How does God guide His people? A thousand different ways. But no matter what form the guidance may take, it will always be 100 percent consistent with the Word of God, because God does not contradict Himself. God's moment-by-moment leading comes through a variety of means. Sometimes through the advice of good Christian friends. Sometimes through prayer. Sometimes by listening to a sermon. Sometimes by an inner conviction that God has spoken to us. Sometimes by a deep sense of inner peace. Sometimes God will guide us through a particular passage of Scripture. Sometimes all of the circumstances of life clearly point in one direction. Sometimes He simply gives us the wisdom to make the right decision. Sometimes He "speaks" to us. Sometimes He guides us by His silence. Very often it is a combination of all of these things put together.

God is committed to guiding His children on their journey from earth to heaven. And though His methods may change, and though sometimes they may be difficult to understand, God is committed to seeing that you ultimately reach your final destination.

LESSON #4:
God's guidance is revealed as we stay close to Him

The Old Testament tells us that the cloud and the pillar represented the very presence of God. They weren't just symbols of some heavenly truth; they represented God's presence with His people. We are told in the Old Testament that the Lord spoke from the cloud. So when they saw the cloud, they understood that the Lord Himself was leading them.

Do you know what that means? If the cloud went north and you went south, you were soon going to get in trouble. If the cloud started moving and your family didn't follow, you would be separated from the presence of God. And the only thing you could do was, turn around and start following the cloud again.

That leads us to a very important conclusion: *God's will is a relationship, not a location.* It is not a question of *where* you should go or *what* you should do. Knowing the will of God is not primarily about who you should marry or when you should get married. It's not about taking this job or that job, or how many kids you should have, or where should you go to school, or whether you should be a missionary or not. Those are secondary questions.

The primary question is this: *are you willing to stay close to God and follow wherever He leads you?* It's a spiritual question. When we say to God, "Show me what to do," the Lord says, "Stay close to Me." We cry out to the heavens, "I'm scared." God says, "Follow Me." We say, "O God, give me some answers." And God says, "Give Me your heart."

That's why Numbers 9:23 says, "At the LORD's command they encamped, and at the LORD's command they set out." If you will do the same thing, God will guide you. If the Lord says stop, you stop. If the Lord says go, you go. He will guide you. The only way to hear God's voice is to stay close to Him. This is a moral and spiritual issue. Are you willing to go when He says go, and are you willing to stop when He says stop? If the answer is yes, you can rest assured that God will guide you exactly where He wants you to go. *The secret of knowing God's will is the secret of knowing God; and as you get to know God better, He will reveal His will to you.*

WHEN YOU NEED TO KNOW, YOU'LL KNOW!

What does that mean for our decision-making? I think it means, *when you need to know, you will know.* If God is God, and if you are committed to knowing Him, staying close to Him, and doing His will, then the ultimate responsibility rests on Him to make His will clear to you.

The issue is not mystical superstition. The issue is, *are you ready to follow God?* If the answer is yes, you may be certain that all your questions about guidance will eventually be answered.

QUESTIONS FOR PERSONAL/GROUP STUDY

1. Sometimes tiny, spur-of-the-moment decisions turn out to have great consequences. Can you think of times in your own experience when what seemed like a small decision at the time came to change your whole life?

2. What is the "romance" of knowing God's will? List several times in your life when you experienced this "romance."

3. How do you feel about the statement that "God wants you to know His will more than you want to know it"? Do you agree with that?

4. If the above statement is true, why do we struggle so often to know God's will?

5. Why does God reveal His will one step at a time instead of all at once? What positive characteristics does the discipline of waiting develop in your life?

6. As you think back to the various turning points of your life, make a list of the different means God has used to reveal His will to you. As you study the list, do you see a pattern in the ways God has guided you?

GOING DEEPER

If you could ask the Lord for specific guidance in any three areas of your life, which areas would you choose? Why? Spend some time in prayer, asking God to give you the guidance you need as you read this book.

CHAPTER TWO

Sense and Nonsense About God's Guidance

In 1988 something new happened in the American political process. That year for the first time ever a televangelist ran for the presidency of the United States.

We all remember that George Bush won the election. But if you roll the tape of your mind backwards—back before the Republican convention, back to the early primaries in New Hampshire and South Carolina, you may recall that Pat Robertson was also a candidate for president.

When Pat Robertson entered the race, there was great furor among the mainstream media in America. How could a preacher, an ordained minister, a televangelist at that, dare to run for President of the United States of America?

For a few months it seemed as if he might actually have a chance to win. Nearly two million people voted for him. By the time of the Republican convention, Pat Robertson, the man the media loved to hate, came in third place behind George Bush and Bob Dole. That would seem to be a good showing for someone who was brand-new on the national political scene.

After the general election ended and George Bush had become president, Pat Robertson set out to write the story of his political campaign from the standpoint of his Christian faith. The

31

book that resulted is actually a book about the will of God and is titled *The Plan*.

BITTERSWEET VICTORY

Everything in that book is colored by Robertson's defeat at the 1988 Republican convention. I was struck by his comments about the strange feeling among his delegates to the convention in New Orleans. On the one hand, they should have been happy because their man had done so well. At last their views were being heard. But the victory was tempered by the undeniable reality that Pat Robertson had come in third. He paints the picture and poses the question this way:

> In the quest for the highest secular prize our nation has to offer, a third place finish is respectable. But my supporters were devastated. It was as if they mourned for the dead. Because they felt—as I did— that God had called me to win, not run third.
>
> So in New Orleans they were asking and I was asking one simple question—did God call me to run for president or not? And if He did call me to run, why did I lose? (*The Plan*, Nashville: Thomas Nelson, 1989, p. 12)

That's really what Pat Robertson's book is all about. How do you explain coming in third when you expected and truly believed that it was God's will for you to win?

"WHAT HAPPENED, LORD?"

It's a common question, isn't it? You set out to get a new job, you work hard for it, you go through the interview process, you do your very best, and in your heart you believe this is the job God wants you to have. Then someone else gets the job. And you say, "Lord, I thought I was doing Your will."

Or perhaps you get the job, and you say, "Thank You, Lord." But six months later you're fired and you say, "What happened, Lord?"

Or you think, "If only we could move to Florida, we would be happy." So you move to Florida, believing it to be the will of God. When you get there, you still are not happy. And you say, "Lord, did we make a mistake?"

Deep in our hearts we know God has a plan for us. We don't debate that; it's not a theological issue with us. We *know* that we weren't put on the earth to grope blindly through the darkness. Nevertheless, that's the way life feels sometimes.

OUR SECRET FEAR

The most fundamental question of life is the one that Saul asked on the road to Damascus: "What shall I do, Lord?" (Acts 22:10). In our better moments, we really want to do what the Lord wants us to do. We really do want to stand before the Lord and hear Him say, "Well done, good and faithful servant."

Many people worry that someday the Lord will say to them, "You did a good job at what you chose to do, but it's not what I sent you to earth to do." Billy Graham said as much to Diane Sawyer in a recent television interview. When she asked him how it felt to be so successful in evangelism, he replied, "I don't feel that way at all. Most of the time I feel like a failure." That's a shocking statement to hear from a man most people would call the greatest Christian leader of our generation. He went on to say that at the age of seventy-five his greatest goal is to someday hear the Lord Jesus say, "Well done, thou good and faithful servant." Then with some diffidence he added, "But I fear I won't hear Him say it."

THE NITTY-GRITTY DETAILS

In the last chapter we discovered that God does indeed desire to guide His children. *If you are willing to follow Him, He will lead you exactly where He wants you to go.* There is nothing controversial about that statement. All Christians would agree with it. The problem comes at the next level—the level of practical application. We know God guides His children, but how does that divine guidance work out in the nitty-gritty details? At precisely this point we need to be very clear in our thinking. There is so much misinformation, so much bad teaching, so much faulty theology when we come to the "how-to" of God's guidance. As a result many Christians continually make wrong turns, go down dead-end streets, and end up in spiritual cul-de-sacs because they don't understand what God has said about the way He guides His children.

In order to help us understand the biblical perspective, I'm going to share four wrong ideas about God's guidance and a biblical answer for each one. Each of these myths, though popular, can be devastating to believers.

MYTH #1:
God wants you to know the future

This myth is listed first because it is the biggest mistake that Christians make with regard to the will of God. *It is the mistake of assuming the end from the beginning.* Because God has led us one step in a particular direction, we assume that the end result must be guaranteed. We start down a road, and because we are going a certain direction we think the destination is certain.

Let's be clear on this one point: *it is rarely God's will for you to know your personal future.* Psalm 119:105 paints a clear picture of how we discover the will of God: "Your word is a lamp to my feet and a light for my path." The picture here is not of a blazing light that illuminates an entire room. It is a picture of a man in total darkness walking along a dangerous trail. There is no moon in the sky. Darkness clings to him. His only light comes from the lantern in his hand. As he holds the lantern, it illuminates the step right in front of him. When he takes that step, what happens to the light? It goes forward one more step. The light is not bright enough to illuminate even ten yards ahead.

Let's face the truth—we want to know the future. At least we think we do. We want to know what is going to happen next year, so we can be ready in advance. But God won't play that game with us.

HE KNOWS—AND HE'S NOT TELLING

The Bible says, "The secret things belong to the LORD our God" (Deuteronomy 29:29). Does He know what will happen tomorrow? Yes, He does; but He's not telling anyone else about it. Or to put it in familiar terms, does God have a blueprint for your life? Yes, He does; but I don't know any way you can get a copy.

A year ago my friend Oceile Poage died of cancer. It started in March when she noticed a stomachache that wouldn't go away. After two or three weeks she went to see a doctor, who put her through a battery of tests but couldn't find anything wrong. Months later the diagnosis was finally confirmed—cancer of the stomach lining. Prognosis: slow death. Her chances of survival: 10 percent. One doctor said he had known two patients out of fifty who had survived this particular type of cancer. If she was lucky, she might live four to six months. When the doctors broke the news, they told her, "We can do chemotherapy, but it will make you very sick and it might not do anything to stop the cancer."

What do you do then? How do you determine God's will? Oceile decided to take chemotherapy as long as she could, but that she would stop if it made her so sick she couldn't enjoy her last days with her family.

As is often the case in these situations, Oceile was more at peace about the future than her family was. They didn't want to talk about death. But Oceile wasn't into avoidance. At one point she told me, "I'm not afraid of the future. If I die, I go to be with Jesus. If I live, I get to spend more time with my family and friends. I win either way."

Despite the doctor's prediction, Oceile made it to Christmas. In an apparently unrelated event, on New Year's Eve some friends called us from Los Angeles to say they had found a special airline ticket offer. They could fly from L.A. to Chicago for $140, but they would have to fly back to Los Angeles within twenty-four hours. Would we like to see them? Of course. So they arrived at 9:48 P.M. one night and flew back at 7:00 P.M. the next day. Crazy? Yes, but it's a good crazy, the kind that says, "I've got a chance to do this now, and I might not have the chance again."

Right after our friends called from Los Angeles, Marlene and I dropped by Oceile's house to bring her a meal. Christmas had been wonderful for her—not least because she had already lived longer than the doctors expected. She found a book about Michael Jordan that she gave my oldest son as a gift. Two days earlier she had visited a huge antique mall in Indiana with her family. She looked great, except that her hair had fallen out and she had lost lots of weight. Her blood count was down; so they postponed chemotherapy for a few days—a fact that greatly pleased her.

A FINAL ACT OF LOVE

"The doctors don't seem to know whether I'm getting better or not. I wish I knew whether I was living or dying," she said. As everyone who knew her could testify, she was very much alive even though she was dying. Several weeks later she flew to Baltimore with her daughter and husband to visit a ninety-nine-year-old woman who was a longtime friend. Oceile brought food to her friend, cooked a meal, then stayed to talk with her because she wanted to make sure her friend knew Jesus Christ. It was Oceile's final act of love; she died several hours after returning to Chicago.

Looking back on her last few weeks, I remembered what her husband said when we told him about our friends flying in from Los Angeles on the spur of the moment. "I think that's the way the Lord wants us to live. Sometimes we wait for our plans to all work out before we do anything. Then it's too late." I don't know whether he would have said that a year ago. Cancer has a way of bringing you face to face with the fact that no one but God knows what the future holds. As for Oceile, her battle with cancer illustrates the fact that you don't have to know the future in order to know God's will. She died as she had lived—serving others. The cancer simply made each day more precious. The lesson is clear: *knowing God's will always involves taking life as it comes, day by day, moment by moment, step by step.*

DOES GOD HAVE A BLUEPRINT OF YOUR LIFE?

That brings us back to the question of the blueprint—the detailed outline of your personal future. Does God have a blueprint that includes everything in your life from the moment of your birth to the moment of your death? Is there a heavenly blueprint that shows what you are supposed to do on October 14, 2003? The answer to that question is, yes. But the only part of it you can see arrives each morning in the form of twenty-four brand-new hours, freshly delivered by United Angel Service Overnight Express.

Please don't miss this point: *God wants to teach us to trust Him step by step*. He reveals His will one step at a time, so we will trust Him moment by moment.

MYTH #2:
God wants you to have 100 percent certainty before you make a decision

Many people believe they must be 100 percent certain of God's will before they make a decision. I can understand their thinking. After all, if you are facing a life-changing decision—a potential marriage, a cross-country move, a new career, which college to attend, whether or not to begin chemotherapy—you'd like to know in advance beyond any doubt that you are doing what God wants you to do.

There are two problems with this point of view. First, sometimes we think we know God's will with 100 percent certainty only to find out later that we were mistaken. Pat Robertson thought it was God's will for him to run *and* win in 1988. Whatever else might be said about his understanding of God's will, we can safely say that his 100 percent certainty didn't equal 100 percent of God's will, since George Bush ended up in the White House.

The other problem—which is more common for most believers—is that in our search for certainty about God's will, we end up paralyzed by an inability to make up our minds. Some decisions are so important they can't be left to chance. As the popular saying goes, "When in doubt, don't." If you aren't sure about the new job, don't take it; don't make the move, don't say yes, don't make any decision with less than total certainty.

But is that good advice? Is it realistic? Is that the way God normally works?

HOW MUCH DID THEY KNOW?

- Did Noah know all about the Flood? No, but he built the ark anyway.
- Did Abraham have a road map? No, but he left Ur of the Chaldees anyway.
- Did Jacob know where he was going? No, but he left home because he couldn't safely stay there.

- Did Moses understand what it meant to lead God's people out of Egypt? No, but he said yes when the Lord called him.

- Did Joshua know how the walls were going to come tumbling down? No, but he marched around Jericho anyway.

- Did Gideon fully grasp God's plan to defeat the Midianites? No, he doubted it from the beginning. But God delivered His people anyway.

- Did young David have a clue of what was to come when Samuel said to Jesse, "This is the one"? No, but the Spirit of the Lord came upon him anyway.

- Did Jehoshaphat know how God was going to defeat the Ammonites? No, but he put the singers at the front of the army and sent them out to battle anyway.

We could add a hundred other examples from the Bible. Did the three Hebrew children know how they would be delivered? Was Daniel totally sure the lions would welcome his dropping in on them? Did Peter know he could walk on water? Did Paul know what would happen when he finally got to Rome?

The answer is always no. *The life of faith means living with uncertainty even in the midst of doing God's will.* That's the whole point of Hebrews 11. Those great men and women didn't know the future, but they trusted God anyway, sometimes in the face of great personal suffering. And because they kept on believing when circumstances turned against them, they received a great reward.

Too many people want what God has never promised—100 percent certainty before they act. So they wait and wait and they dilly and they dally and they stop and they hesitate and they ruminate. They refuse to go forward because they are waiting for 100 percent certainty. That leads me to this important observation: *it is rarely God's will to give you 100 percent certainty before you make an important decision.*

LOOKING FOR "THE MAN"

We see this principle vividly illustrated in Acts 16. When the Apostle Paul and his team left Troas, they sailed across the Aegean Sea in response to a vision of a man saying, "Come over to

Macedonia and help us" (v. 9). When they got there, they found a woman named Lydia. But what about "the man"? He was nowhere to be found. Later on Paul and Silas were arrested, stripped, flogged, and thrown in jail. That night during an earthquake, they led their jailer to Christ, then baptized him and his whole family. The next morning Paul and Silas were released and escorted out of the city by the town leaders, who were glad to see them go.

It's a strange story. In many ways it appears that Paul failed in Philippi. After all, he was in trouble almost from the moment he arrived. Where is the great church he came to establish?

But from God's point of view Paul did exactly what he should have done. He followed God's leading—God gave more light—Paul took another step and waited for further developments. Step by step, through twists and turns and unexpected means, Paul did what God wanted him to do, even though it wasn't what he expected to do when he arrived in town.

TROUBLE IN PARADISE

After sharing these insights with my congregation, I received a letter from a close friend who lives down the street from us. After much planning and prayer and after many frustrating delays, she and her husband recently moved into an older house only to discover that it was in much worse shape than they had expected, costing them many thousands of dollars to restore. They also had a long series of unpleasant encounters with a cantankerous neighbor. Looking back on all the difficulties, my friend penned these words:

> Seeking God's will has never caused me much difficulty in the past (partly because I didn't always!), but when we were in the throes of trying to decide about buying this house, we both prayed long and hard that we would have a clear sense of direction and guidance from the Lord or at least a sense of peace about a decision if it were the right one.
>
> Because of the many troubles we've had while living here, I had convinced myself that we made the wrong decision and were paying for it in a big way. Resentment started to taint my relationship with God. Why would He allow us to make such a terrible

mistake (expensive one too!) when we spent so much time asking Him for His guidance?

Only in the last few weeks have I felt that God does indeed want us here. Our difficulties in getting in here were not God slamming the door shut, but rather Him holding it open just wide enough for us to squeeze through. Our difficulties in buying the house now seem like good training for the battles while we're in it. Your example from Acts reinforced in my mind this idea and the wrong thinking that was giving me the resentment: that the outcome does not retroactively affect whether it was God's will!

That final sentence is crucial. "The outcome does not retroactively affect whether it was God's will." That's exactly right. *Doing God's will means taking the next step—whatever it is—without a definite promise about the end result.* Many times you won't have 100 percent certainty; but when the moment comes to decide, you must make the best decision you can, trusting God for the results. Sometimes you'll know more, sometimes less; but living by faith means taking the next step anyway.

MYTH #3:
God's highest goal is my happiness

Millions of people buy into this false idea. They believe that their happiness is God's supreme goal for them. That sounds good, doesn't it? "God wants me to be happy." "God wants me to be fulfilled." "God wants me to be successful." That thinking has been used to justify all kinds of bizarre and even evil behavior. Some Christian men have said, "It is God's will that I should divorce my wife and marry another woman because we are in love, and God wants us to be happy." The correct theological term for that is, "Baloney."

NOT HAPPY BUT HOLY

If your personal happiness is not God's highest goal for you, then what is God's will for your life? *It is God's will for you to be holy.* It is God's will for you to be like Jesus Christ. It is God's will for you to be in a place of maximum usefulness for the kingdom of God.

First Thessalonians 4:3 states this plainly: "It is God's will that you should be holy" [some translations say, "sanctified"]. To be "sanctified" means to be made holy. It refers to the life-long process whereby God shapes you, through a myriad of experiences both positive and negative, into the image of Jesus Christ. Here's the clincher: *He uses the very worst things that happen to us in order to accomplish His divine purposes in us.*

"SHE'S STILL MY WIFE"

A close friend of mine found himself put to the test in the last four years. After many happy years of marriage, his wife suddenly developed Alzheimer's disease. Her descent from rationality happened so fast that even the doctors were surprised. At first my friend hired a housekeeper to take care of his wife, but that solution did not work for long. Soon he admitted her to a nursing home with a special unit for patients with Alzheimer's.

The first time he took me to visit her, I was not prepared for what I saw. The woman I had known—vibrant and full of life—had simply disappeared. In her place was a feeble old woman barely able to feed herself. But when we walked in, she recognized her husband and called him by name. We walked arm-in-arm down the hall together, listening to her chatter away aimlessly, her words and sentences tumbling out unconnected as if some inner computer had been tampered with and the wires hopelessly crossed. Toward the end of our visit, when her husband asked if she would like me to pray for her, she said, "Yes, that would be nice," then stared blankly into space while I prayed.

As we left to go home, we got into separate cars. My friend brushed the tears from his eyes before he drove away.

But that is only part of the story. My friend also has a very successful career that takes him around the world. More than that, his work repeatedly puts him in business meetings at some of the most glamorous resort areas known to man. He is strong, has a charismatic personality, is visibly successful, and is one of the most respected men in his field. By the world's standards, he has it all.

I asked him at one point why he remained faithful to his marriage vows. There was no chance—none whatsoever—that his wife would get better.

"I MADE A PROMISE"

"Simple. I made a promise, and I have to keep it. Years ago when I pledged to be faithful to my wife, I didn't know she would have Alzheimer's disease. But she made the same promise to me. It could have happened to me instead of her. As a Christian, I simply have no choice but to be faithful no matter what happens."

Lest that sound grim and hopeless, he added these words: "Since my wife has developed Alzheimer's disease, I have gone through the hardest time of my life. Yet out of that hard time, God has drawn me closer to Himself than I've ever been before. If I were unfaithful, I would lose all I have gained in my walk with the Lord. I would be a double loser then.

"My wife," he continued, "is contributing all she can to the marriage. The fact that she's locked up for her own safety doesn't change that fact. Even though she barely recognizes me now, we're still married. I've made a promise to her, and I'm going to keep it."

"MY SON HAS BEEN WATCHING YOU"

Several years have passed since he said those words. Before she died, his wife regressed to the point where she no longer could communicate with anyone. In the end she sat motionless in a chair, her hands clenched, her legs permanently crossed. The doctors have no idea what kept her alive so long except that somewhere deep inside her a spark of life kept burning. One day her husband said to me, "I don't know why she is still alive. I can't see any purpose in it. Why is God allowing her to hang on when the person I knew disappeared years ago?" My friend wasn't complaining, but just stating the facts as he saw them. He was still faithful, but the road was hard, the nights long, the loneliness intense, the future bleak.

Then my friend spent an evening with a man who told him, "You'll never know what you have meant to my son. He's been watching you take care of your wife all these years. You don't know it, but he's been talking about you to everyone he meets. He tells them that anyone else would have left her by now and started a new life. But you didn't do that. You stayed with her. And that has made a profound impression on my son."

My friend told me, "Maybe that's it. Maybe God allowed this so that somehow through it all I could help someone else."

Nothing I have said can lessen the terrible pain my friend endured. But he would tell you that God has changed his life profoundly through the experience of watching his wife die. He would also say that God has seen fit to use this to reach many people for Jesus Christ.

Is my friend happy? That depends on the circumstances of any given day. But there is unmistakable joy in spite of everything and a hard-won faith in the goodness of God.

With that, we come to the final myth.

MYTH #4:
God makes His will hard to find

Many people struggle unnecessarily in this area. Perhaps they are seeking 100 percent certainty, or maybe they are seeking some kind of message from God—a postcard that reads, "Dear Jack, Buy the red Pontiac. Signed, God." Or they fear that one night, while they are watching *Monday Night Football*, God will reveal His will, and they will somehow miss it. Or they worry that they have sinned too much and have blown their only chance to do God's will.

"TRUST ME"

To all these things God says, "Trust Me." *God wants you to know His will more than you want to know it.* God is more committed to showing you His will than you are to discovering it. He takes full responsibility for getting you from here to there step by step. He has said, "Never will I leave you" (Hebrews 13:5). And He won't. He also said, "I will instruct you and teach you in the way you should go" (Psalm 32:8). And He will. He also promised, "Surely I will be with you always" (Matthew 28:20). And He is.

We think that God's will is hard to find. The biblical perspective is quite different. *God will reveal His will to anyone who is willing to do it*. That leads me to one final thought: *God ordinarily will not show you His will in order for you to consider it*. He won't show you His will so you can say, "Maybe I will . . . maybe I won't. How about Plan B, Lord?" He will show you His will when He knows you are willing to do it.

John 7:17 makes this truth very plain. Jesus said to the Jews, "If anyone chooses to do God's will, he will find out whether my teaching comes from God or whether I speak on my own." Concentrate on that first phrase—"If anyone chooses to do God's will." You have to choose before you know. If you want to know God's will, you have to choose to do it before you know what it is. You don't say, "Lord, You show me, and then I'll decide what I am going to do." The Lord says, "No, you decide to obey Me, and then I will show you what I want you to do."

Let me boil it down to one rather astounding statement: *if you are willing to do God's will, you will do it*. The only thing that is required is a total willingness on your part to do God's will, and you will do it. Step by step. Moment by moment. Day by day. If you are willing to do God's will, you will do it because He will see to it.

Is that easy? Yes and no. It's not easy because everything in this world pulls you away from God. But it is easy in the sense that you can truly do God's will if you want to.

That leaves us with two penetrating questions. First, *do you want to know God's will?* If the answer is no or if you are not sure, then let me ask the second question: *are you willing to be made willing?* Maybe that's where we need to end this chapter. Are you willing to be made willing? If you will say, "Lord, I am not sure I am willing, but I am willing to be made willing," He will lead you step by step. If you are willing to do His will, you will do it.

QUESTIONS FOR PERSONAL/GROUP STUDY

1. Why is it important that you ask God for guidance? What happens when you skip this important first step?

2. List three times in your life when you—like Pat Robertson—thought you understood God's will only to find out later that things didn't work out exactly as you expected. Why does God let that happen to us from time to time?

3. How do you feel about the statement, "It is rarely God's will for you to know your personal future"? Does that discourage you in any way? Suppose you had known in advance everything that was going to happen to you in the last ten years. How would that knowledge have changed your life? Suppose God offered to show you the next ten years in detail. Would you take Him up on that offer? Why or why not?

4. True or False: God wants you to know His will more than you want to know it.

True or False: God wants you to struggle to know His will.

True or False: Great men and women of faith never struggle over God's will.

5. How do you feel about the statement, "If you are willing to do God's will, you will do it"?

6. What is the Number One factor keeping you from doing God's will right now? Is there something holding you back? What is it?

GOING DEEPER

Make a list of the five biggest decisions you've made in your life. Next to each decision, write yes or no to this question: at the time, did you believe you were doing God's will? Then write a sentence or two giving your long-range evaluation of how that decision turned out. What conclusions do you draw about the way God works in your life?

CHAPTER THREE

The Incredible Journey

I t is sometimes said that a crisis never makes a man—it only reveals what he already is. That thought is both comforting and frightening because we all wonder how we would react if everything we held dear was really on the line.

Our family . . .
Our health . . .
Our career . . .
Our future . . .
Our life . . .

We wonder, would we have the faith to make it? Or would we collapse? All the things we say we believe—would they still be enough when the crunch comes?

In the Bible there is a chapter written about the men and women whose faith was strong in times of crisis. The names written there are like a biblical hall of fame: Abel . . . Enoch . . . Noah . . . Abraham . . . Sarah . . . Jacob . . . Joseph . . . Moses . . . Joshua . . . David. Different people, different stories, widely separated in time and space. Stories that span thousands of years. Stories that encompass murder, natural catastrophe, family treachery, physical weakness, failed dreams, missed opportunities, sibling rivalry, and military conquest. The men and women whose stories are told in this particular chapter differ in every way but one: *what they did, they did by faith*.

So when the crisis came, it did not make them—it only revealed what they already were.

That chapter is Hebrews 11.

THE MAN FROM NIGERIA

Some years ago I pastored a church in Garland, Texas, a suburb on the northeast side of Dallas. Because of our location and our unofficial connection with Dallas Theological Seminary, a steady stream of students attended the church. The most unusual seminary student I ever met came to us late one summer. At the time I did not know him or his story. He had traveled from Nigeria with his wife and six children to study at the seminary, hoping someday to return to his homeland to serve as a leader of the New Salem Church. When I met him, Lekan Olatoye was forty-four years old.

I noticed at once that he was very friendly. He and his wife and their children fit right in. In the course of time he helped out around the church. When we discovered he had a knack for things electrical, we put him to work repairing the many broken fixtures in the building we were renting. Later he and Irene taught Sunday school to the toddlers. He signed up to take Evangelism Explosion. Many Tuesday nights we visited new residents in Garland, inviting them to our church and (whenever we got the chance) sharing the Gospel. I can remember the night Lekan shared his testimony during a visit. He told of coming to Christ out of an animistic background, of a radical conversion experience that completely changed the direction of his life. The precise details escape me, but the image of joy inscribed on his face remains in my mind across the years. That year at Christmastime when Marlene and I had an open house, our friend's whole family came. I can still see all eight of them sitting in a row on a couch in our living room.

A few months later we had a men's retreat at Pine Cove in east Texas. That Friday night Lekan joined in our air-hockey competition. The next morning we had a sports tournament, and he joined right in. He took notes during the morning Bible study. And that afternoon, about 2:15 P.M., I passed him as he was going to the pool, a towel draped casually around his neck. He went swimming and then joined a lazy game of volleyball.

NO MIRACLE THAT DAY

Suddenly he pitched forward and fell to the ground, his glasses flying from his face. The other men thought he had fainted from overexertion, but when they could get no pulse, it was clear that something terrible had happened. A cry for help went out, and a paramedic who was with us administered CPR. Men gathered in groups to pray. At length an ambulance came and took him away.

But there was to be no miracle that day. In truth, he was dead before he hit the ground. It was a stroke or perhaps a massive heart attack.

We gathered our things and went back to Dallas. I have faced many difficult tasks as a pastor, but the hardest thing I have ever done was to tell that sweet wife she no longer had a husband and to tell those dear children they no longer had a father.

I pondered that day—and many days since—what it all meant. A man in the prime of his life leaves his country, his home, his job and goes overseas to study God's Word. He means to return to his own people someday. His only purpose in going is to fulfill God's will for his life. He has no other motive. At enormous personal sacrifice, he walks away from a lucrative career and takes his family halfway around the world.

Then he is cut down at the age of forty-four before he even gets started.

What does it all mean? Why would God allow such a thing to happen to a man dedicated to doing His will? And in a larger sense, what does such a tragedy teach us about discovering and doing God's will ourselves?

In order to understand the answer to that question, I would like to focus our attention on Hebrews 11. Not on the whole chapter but on one man, Abraham. And not his whole story, but the record of his incredible journey to the Promised Land. The long version of Abraham's life is given in Genesis; the Hebrews passage is the short summary. Hebrews 11:8-10 tells of one man who obeyed God's call at great personal sacrifice. It tells us what he did; more importantly, it tells us why he did it.

A PLACE CALLED UR

Let's begin with some brief facts about Abraham. When we meet him in the Bible, he is living 4,000 years ago in a far-off place called Ur of the Chaldees—on the banks of the Euphrates River, not far from the mouth of the Persian Gulf. No doubt he and his wife Sarah worship the moon-god Sin. He is a prosperous, middle-aged man, successful by any human standard. Life has been good to Abraham and Sarah. Certainly they have no reason to complain.

It is at precisely this moment that God speaks to him—clearly, definitely, unmistakably. What God says will change his life—and ultimately alter the course of world history.

TRUTH #1:
Living by faith means accepting God's call without knowing where it will lead

> By faith Abraham, when called to go to a place he would later receive as his inheritance, obeyed and went, even though he did not know where he was going (Hebrews 11:8).

There is only one way to describe Ur of the Chaldees. It was a world-class city. Archaeologists tell us that in Abraham's day perhaps 250,000 people lived there. It was a center of mathematics, astronomy, commerce, and philosophy. People from outlying areas moved to Ur because they wanted to be part of that great city.

No doubt many of Abraham's friends thought he was crazy. Why would anyone want to leave Ur? Obeying God's call meant giving up his friends, his career, his traditions, his home, his position, his influence, and his country. More than that, it meant risking his health and his future on a vague promise from an unseen God to lead him to "a land that I will show you."

When Abraham left Ur, he burned his bridges behind him. For him there could be no turning back. Once he left the walls of Ur, he was on his own, following God's call into the unknown.

You say, "He gave all that up?"

"Yes."

"That's kind of strange, isn't it?"

"Is it?"

Please don't miss the point. *When God calls, there are no guarantees about tomorrow.* Abraham truly didn't know where he was going, didn't know how he would get there, didn't know how long it would take, and didn't even know for sure how he would know he was there when he got there. All he knew was that God had called him. Period. Everything else was up in the air.

You want a long life? So do I.

You want to rise in your profession? So do I.

You want lots of friends? So do I.

You want to grow old and die with your family around you? So do I.

There's nothing wrong with those desires. All of us feel that way. But living by faith means no guarantees and no certainty about the future.

If you truly want to do God's will, sometimes you will find yourself exactly where Abraham was—setting out on a new journey that doesn't seem to make sense from the world's point of view. This touches the point we raised in the last chapter about the impossibility of being 100 percent certain in advance. Do you think Abraham was 100 percent certain? Not a chance. The only certainty he had was that God had called him and that he must obey. The rest was shrouded in mystery. That fact makes his obedience all the more impressive. Hebrews 11:8 says he "obeyed and went." There was no greater miracle in his life than that. Everything else that happened flowed from this basic decision. *God called; he obeyed.* That truth was the secret of his life. He stepped out in faith even though there were no guarantees about his own personal future.

You see a man at 2:15 P.M. and he's fine. By 3 P.M. he's dead. What does that mean? Was his faith weak? No. Had he sinned? No. Was he somehow out of God's will? No. Did God make a mistake? No. Did God break His promise? No. Did my friend plan to die that day? Absolutely not.

Let me put it another way: *living by faith means stepping out for God and leaving the results to Him.* It's no guarantee of long life and good success. You may have those blessings. But you may not.

The life of faith means, "I am going to be the man or woman God wants me to be, no matter where it leads. I don't know the future, but I'm trusting Him to work out the details. In the meantime, I step out by faith and follow where He leads me."

That brings us to the second great truth about living by faith.

TRUTH #2:
Living by faith means waiting on God to keep His promises

> By faith he made his home in the promised land like a stranger in a foreign country; he lived in tents, as did Isaac and Jacob, who were heirs with him of the same promise (Hebrews 11:9).

There is within all of us a natural desire to settle down. Earlier in this book I have written about the travail of selling our present home and buying another. Even though we are only moving a few miles, the entire experience has been traumatic and disruptive. The older I get, the less I like to move. I value coming home to the same place and the same faces every day. Even as I write these words, our home is filled with boxes waiting to be transported to our new house. To me, it is unsettling to look at bare walls that only a few days ago were covered with familiar pictures. Suddenly this home looks less like a home and more like a building where we used to live in some distant past. And when I drove past our new house today, it didn't yet register as "home." The whole experience leaves me with a vague sense of uneasiness, of homelessness if you will.

Multiply that feeling by a factor of 100 and spread it out over fifty years and you approximate Abraham's situation as he came to the Promised Land. Our text tells us that he "lived in tents." I know lots of people who like to camp on vacation, but I don't know anyone who voluntarily lives in a tent as a permanent residence. Tents speak of impermanence, of the possibility of moving on at any moment, of the fact that you live on land you do not personally own.

That's Abraham. He didn't own anything in the Promised Land. God had promised to give him the land; yet he lived like "a stranger in a foreign country." If you don't own the land, you can't build a permanent dwelling there.

In many ways this is even more remarkable than leaving Ur in the first place. As long as he was traveling across the desert, he could dream about the future. But when he got to Canaan, all illusions disappeared. Think of what he didn't find:

- No "Welcome, Abraham" sign.

- No discount coupons from the merchants.

- No housewarming party.

- No visit from the Welcome Wagon.

- No mayor with the key to the city.

- No band playing "Happy Days Are Here Again."

- No ticker-tape parade.

Nobody expected him. Nobody cared that he had come. Nobody gave him anything.

God had promised him the land . . . but he had to scratch out an existence in tents. Hundreds of years would pass before the promise was completely fulfilled. Abraham never saw it happen. Neither did Isaac or Jacob.

Was Abraham in the will of God? Yes. Was he right to leave Ur? Yes. Was he doing what God wanted him to do? Yes. Why, then, was he living in tents? Because God's timetable is not the same as ours. He's not in a big hurry like we are. God works across the generations to accomplish His purposes; we're worried about which dress or shirt to buy for the big party this weekend. There is a big difference in those two perspectives.

A third principle at work in Abraham's life is the ultimate key to the life of faith.

TRUTH #3:
Living by faith means never taking
your eyes off heaven

For he was looking forward to the city with foundations, whose architect and builder is God (Hebrews 11:10).

Abraham looked for a "city with foundations"—that is, for a "*city*," not a lonely spot in the desert. He wanted to live in a place filled with other people. He also looked for a city with "*foundations*," a place with security and permanence that could not be found in a tent. That meant he was looking for a city designed and built by God. Why? Because all earthly cities eventually crumble to dust.

Not long ago I visited the ruins of the ancient city of Jericho. When most people think of Jericho, they think of the city whose walls came tumbling down in the days of Joshua. But that's only *one* Jericho. Archaeologists have discovered *layers* of Jericho, one after another, the city having been built, destroyed, and rebuilt across the centuries. The same is true of Jerusalem. When you visit Old Jerusalem, you aren't exactly "walking where Jesus walked." You are actually walking thirty to seventy-five feet *above* where Jesus walked. According to one source, Jerusalem has been destroyed and rebuilt at least forty-seven times in the last 3,500 years.

That's the way it is with all earthly cities. Nothing built by man lasts forever. No wonder Abraham was looking for a city built and designed by God.

Revelation 21 describes that city as "the New Jerusalem, coming down out of heaven from God" (v. 2). In his vision John saw a city of breathtaking beauty, shining with the glory of God, "and its brilliance was like that of a very precious jewel, like a jasper, clear as crystal" (v. 11). Christians have always looked to the New Jerusalem as the final abode for the people of God, the place where we will spend eternity together in the presence of the Lord. But note this: heaven is a *city*. It's a real place filled with real people. That's the city Abraham was looking for when he left Ur of the Chaldees.

Abraham was going to heaven, and he knew it. *That one fact—and that alone—explains his life.* He had his heart set on heaven, and that explains why he could:

- Leave the beautiful city of Ur.
- Walk away from his career.
- Leave his friends far behind.
- Live in tents until the end of his life.
- Start all over again in a new land.
- Die without seeing all that God had promised.

Abraham knew he was going to heaven, and that changed his whole perspective on life. He knew not just that he was going to die, but that after death he was going to enter a city God had designed and made.

IS HE CRAZY?

So here's a nice man in his early forties. He has a good job and a great future. He's on the fast track to the top of his field. In a nation where so many live in poverty, he has a nice house, a lovely wife, and six wonderful children. It's a great situation.

One day God says, "I want you to go to America and learn to preach the Word." "Are You talking to me, Lord?" "Yes, I'm talking to you."

When he tells his wife, she says, "Whatever you say, honey." They sell everything and come to America though people back home beg him to stay. They just shake their heads when he says he is following the call of God.

So what do you think? Is he crazy? Has he lost it? No; he's found it.

He comes because he knows he's going to heaven someday . . . so it doesn't matter so much where he lives in the meantime.

He doesn't plan to die at forty-four. No one ever does. But that's all right too. Because he knows he's going to heaven when he dies.

"DID WE DO RIGHT?"

The night Lekan died, I went to his house to deliver the sad news. His family and I talked a long time, and his wife, Irene, told me this story: "When he decided to come to America, he told his boss what he was going to do. They didn't want him to leave, so they came to me and said, 'Tell him to stay. Tell him if he stays, we'll make him a General Manager.'"

They came anyway.

That night, looking back, she said, "Did we do right? We came, and he died. Now we're here in America, and he is dead. Did we do right?"

The number two daughter, a seventh-grader, immediately said, "Yes."

"Yes. Better to die as a seminary student than to be General Manager in Nigeria," Irene said.

That, I think, is what the life of faith is all about. It's a decision to live your life in a different way. It's a conscious choice to live for eternity and not for this present life. Please understand: it is *not* idle resignation to martyrdom or suffering. It is a personal choice to follow wherever God leads.

After Lekan died, we discovered a great deal about him we hadn't known before. When he converted from Islam, he dedicated his life to the service of Jesus Christ. And so, for the ten years before he came to America, he had asked to be transferred to various stations across Nigeria so that he could plant churches wherever he worked.

When he came, it was as the hope of his church. He represented the future for the New Salem Church of Nigeria. He would be the anchor for a seminary that would prepare men to preach the Word of God.

DEATH OF A THOUSAND DREAMS

Now he was dead at the age of forty-four, leaving behind a wife and six children. When Lekan died, a thousand dreams died with him. He was the first international student ever to die while enrolled at Dallas Seminary. There was no one from Nigeria to take his place. What would the Nigerians do? How would the church go on? It looked like Satan had won the battle.

A few months later the Nigerians sent two men to visit us in

Texas—Pastor Julian and Dr. Jones Fatunwase, the General Superintendent of the New Salem Church. They came halfway around the world just to thank us for what we had done.

At the end of the week, just before I took them to the airport, I said, "Tell me something—is the church in Nigeria stronger or is it weaker now that Lekan has died? You sent him over here, and he died in the middle of his studies. How is the church doing?"

The answer came quickly. "Don't you understand? The church is so much stronger now." "How so?" I asked. "When we had the funeral, 10,000 people came from all over Nigeria," Dr. Fatunwase replied. And one of those at the funeral was Lekan's older brother Dele. He was not a Christian. Lekan had prayed for him for ten years. At that funeral, to use my new friend's exact words, Dele Olatoye "decided for Jesus Christ."

In addition, Dr. Fatunwase said, "There were so many people in our churches who had grown complacent." They thought it wasn't that important to live for the Lord. But when they heard how Lekan had died—to use his exact words once again—"a glorious death serving the Lord, hundreds of our people learned it's not how *long* you live, but how *well* you live. Our church in Nigeria is much, much stronger now," he concluded.

"DIED AT TWENTY-FIVE, BURIED AT SEVENTY-FIVE"

How long do you expect to live? To put it more pointedly, how many more years do you think you have left before someone holds your funeral service? Ten years? Twenty years? Thirty years? Forty years? Fifty years? Sixty years? How much of that time are you sure of? The last question is easy. You're not sure about any of it. The truth is, you could die tomorrow—or today—from any of a thousand causes. No one knows how long he or she will live or precisely when he or she will die.

It's not how long you live that matters, but what you do with the years you are given. Too many people die at age twenty-five but aren't buried until they are seventy-five. They waste their best years in trivial pursuits, all the while missing out on the excitement of living by faith.

TWO KINDS OF SUCCESS

Here is the whole chapter in one sentence: *following God's will doesn't guarantee worldly success.* The operative word is "worldly." God has one view of success; the world has another. Joshua 1:8 reminds us that those who meditate on God's Word will be "prosperous and successful." Psalm 1 contrasts the fool who looks to the wicked for advice with the godly who builds his life on the Word of God. The latter will be like "a tree planted by streams of waters." God rewards such a man in this way: "Whatever he does prospers" (v. 3).

But let's not confuse that with the false notion that doing God's will leads to a trouble-free life. Abraham lived in tents all his life. He died without receiving all that God had promised to him. In many ways you could say that by leaving he forfeited any chance at worldly greatness. Never again would he know the stability and settled prosperity that he had in Ur. From the day he left until the day he died, Abraham was a sojourner, a tent-dweller, a man living on land he did not own.

"THAT'S CRAZY!"

Some time ago a friend called me to talk about a sermon he had heard that tremendously upset him. In the course of the sermon the preacher illustrated his remarks with a story about his decision to go to seminary. He was older than the normal age and had already built a thriving business. After sending in his application, he decided to take a step of faith. He sold his business, moved to a distant city, and invested all his life savings in buying a house. All this without knowing whether or not he would be accepted. At length his faith was rewarded when he was accepted by the seminary. That's the whole story. To me, it didn't seem very unusual. People do that kind of thing all the time. What surprised me was my friend's reaction to that illustration. To say he was furious would understate the matter. I have never known him to be so upset. "How could anyone do something as stupid as that?" he shouted over the telephone. "That's not faith. That's forcing God's hand." Then he added this comment: "Sure, it worked out for him. But what about all the others who tried it and it didn't work?"

Good question. On one hand, I think my friend was revealing more about himself and his need for earthly security than about the wisdom or folly of what the preacher did. I've heard similar stories many times—most of them with relatively happy endings. On the other hand, he does raise a good point. There are times when people take a major step of faith only to find that it backfires on them. What if the man hadn't been accepted at seminary? Well, I suppose he would have put his skills to work finding a job in the new city or perhaps he would have decided to move back where he came from. No shame there. But wouldn't that prove that he was wrong about God's will? No, not necessarily. I've already pointed out that nothing worked out for Abraham quite the way he might have expected when he left Ur.

And what about my friend who after a lifetime in Chicago is moving his whole family to another city to start all over again? He and I have already discussed the possibility that things might not work out for him the way he hopes they will. But that's not stopping him from taking the step of faith. I say, bully for him. As much as I might prefer that he stay right where he is, I can hardly stand in the way of a man who truly wants to follow the Lord and is willing to take an unusual step even though things might not work out. No matter what happens, my friend will emerge (I hope and believe) from this experience with a deeper confidence in God because he will be cast upon the Almighty in ways he has never yet known. Either way I think he's going to be all right. But that doesn't preclude some very difficult, scary days of uncertainty as he begins a new life in a new city.

If you ever decide to make God's will the great priority of your life, you will discover that it is indeed an incredible journey. Like Abraham of old, your search for God's will will lead you out of your comfort zone into the exciting arena of living by faith. Along the way, you will discover that you can indeed survive without absolute certainty about what tomorrow will bring. You may even learn to enjoy living on the edge between faith and absolute disaster. In any case, knowing God's will will cease to be an academic exercise, like doing your homework before going to bed at night. Instead, it will become the most exciting adventure you've ever known as you set out into the unknown to follow God wherever He leads you.

QUESTIONS FOR PERSONAL/GROUP STUDY

1. Ponder Abraham's dilemma when the Lord called him to leave Ur of the Chaldees. List as many reasons as you can think of why he might have decided not to obey God's call.

2. Do you consider yourself a risk-taker? Why or why not? How do you think you would have responded if you had been in Abraham's shoes?

3. God "called" Abraham to leave Ur. Do you believe He "calls" people in the same way today? What guidelines do you personally follow in order to determine God's "call" versus your own desires?

4. As you consider the story of Lekan Olatoye, do you know similar stories of others who suffered or died in their attempts to follow God's will? How do you personally react to examples like that? What lessons do you learn?

5. Why is a strong belief in heaven an important part of living by faith and doing God's will?

6. How do you feel about the statement that "faith doesn't always mean having 100 percent certainty"? Have you ever come to a major decision and taken a step of faith in spite of your doubts? What happened?

GOING DEEPER

Think about your own life for a moment. Where do you need to take decisive action? What holds you back? Write down three areas that need genuine change. Jot down one simple step you could take in each area this week. Then pray this simple prayer: "Lord, I want to follow where You are leading. Grant me courage to step out in faith this week. Amen."

CHAPTER FOUR

Who's the Boss?

The voice on the other end of the phone said, "Pastor Ray, I need to talk to you." It was an old friend from Texas who was visiting his wife's family in Indiana. Could they come by and see us? Yes, of course, we'd be delighted. My friend said he had a big decision to make, and he needed some advice.

I remembered another time four or five years earlier when my friend had come to me with another big decision. Back then he was enrolled in a Master's degree program at a university in the Dallas area. But times were tough; he was out of work and almost out of money. Should he drop out of the program? I asked him one question: what do you want to do with your life? When he told me, the answer was easy. Stay in school; do whatever it takes to get your degree; it can only help you get to where you want to go.

In time he got his Master's degree. Still later he became a policeman. He was—and is—a cop. Not just a policeman. My friend is a cop's cop. Tough, no-nonsense, exactly the kind of guy you would want as a partner if you were a policeman and your next call was a drug bust in south Dallas.

Eventually he began to pursue the last part of his dream. He entered a Ph.D. program in criminal justice at one of the best universities in America.

Taking that step required an enormous sacrifice. He worked five days a week as a policeman, sometimes worked a second job, and often attended classes the final two days of the week. It was not easy, and he didn't see his kids or his wife as much as he—or they—wanted.

"I'M THINKING ABOUT QUITTING"

When he came to see me, he was a third of the way through the program and was finding it far tougher than he imagined, even though he had made all A's and one B. He was thinking about quitting because the sacrifice was too great.

When I asked if he had a computer to help him write his papers, he said no, he didn't, partly because of the cost and partly because he didn't want to buy a computer if he was going to drop out of the program.

As we talked, I sensed he had come to a major crossroads. If he dropped out, he would forever give up the dream. But in order for him to stay in the program, he needed a new vision to make the enormous sacrifice worthwhile.

The turning point came when I asked him how his professors had reacted to his Christian faith. "God has given me favor in their eyes, and every one of them has thanked me for bringing that perspective to my course work," he said.

When I heard that, I slammed my hand on the table and exclaimed, "I know exactly what God wants you to do."

CROSSING THE LINE

Before going on with the story, let's travel back twenty centuries to hear the words of Jesus. The place is Caesarea Philippi, a Roman city located in the Golan Heights, northeast of the Sea of Galilee. A huge rock cliff dominates the landscape. At the base of the cliff a stream flows on its way toward the Jordan River.

It is a critical moment for Jesus. All of Israel buzzes with word of this man from Galilee. Who is He? By what power does He perform His miracles? What is He really after? After a wave of early popularity, the nation is now divided. True, He has a wide following among the common people. It is also true that among the rich and powerful, opinion is slowly crystallizing against Him. In the distance, the drums of angry opposition are beginning to beat. Before too many months, their sound will become a deafening roar.

Knowing all this, and knowing that it will end in His death, Jesus gathers His disciples in this quiet place to draw out of them a deeper commitment than they have yet given. Jesus looked ahead to the moment He would hang on a Roman cross. What would happen then? Would these men—his inner circle, the men with whom He had spent so much time—stand by Him or would they fall away? Jesus knew the fickleness of the human heart. He also knew that despite their brave words, none of these men could imagine the road they were about to travel together.

It was time to choose sides. These were handpicked men. Jesus had personally trained them. They knew Him better than anyone else on earth. They had seen Him work miracles, watched Him heal the sick, marveled as He confounded the Pharisees. But had they grasped the meaning of it all?

Jesus had to know the answer. It is here—at Caesarea Philippi—that Jesus asks the question, "Who do people say I am?" (Mark 8:27). And it is here that Peter gives his confession: "You are the Christ, the Son of the living God" (Matthew 16:16).

But the conversation does not end there, for Jesus is seeking more than a *confession*; He is also seeking a *commitment*. "Now that you know who I am, are you willing to commit your life to Me?" This is how Jesus puts the issue before the disciples:

> "If anyone would come after me, he must deny himself and take up his cross and follow me. For whoever wants to save his life will lose it, but whoever loses his life for me and for the gospel will save it. What good is it for a man to gain the whole world, yet forfeit his soul? Or what can a man give in exchange for his soul?" (Mark 8:34-37).

WHAT'S THE BEST DEAL?

Take a careful look at those verses. Twice the text uses the word "life," and twice it uses the word "soul." But in the Greek those are not different words. The Greek word is *psyche*, from which we get our English word *psychology*. Sometimes it refers to the immaterial part of man (his soul) as opposed to his body. But more often it refers to the whole man or to the inner, conscious self we call the personality. The *psyche* is the "real you" that lives and breathes and makes decisions. "Life" is not a bad translation so long as we remember that it means more than just physical existence.

With that as background, we may paraphrase these verses—and add a bit of twentieth-century idiom—in this way:

"Now that you know who I am, are you ready to take up your cross and follow Me? Before you answer, let Me warn you that to follow Me will seem in the eyes of the world as if you are wasting your life. The people of the world will never understand what you are doing. It will seem to them that by following Me, you are throwing your life away.

"You always have another option. You can try to save your own life by following your own desires. Lots of people do that. They live as if their career is all that matters. But the people who live only for this life in the end will find that they wasted it on things that don't really matter. They tried to save it by living for themselves, but in the end they will lose it. They have wasted their lives on trivial pursuits.

"But if you follow Me—though the way will not be easy and you will often be misunderstood—in the end you will save your life. And the people who laugh at you now will not laugh at you then. They will see that you were right and they were wrong.

"After all, what good will it do if you become the richest man in the world or climb to the top of the corporate ladder or rise to the highest salary level in your company or win the applause of the world—what good will all that do if in the end you find out it was all wasted? What good will that shiny, new sports car do you then? Will you be able to trade it in for another life? No, you won't. But if you want to live that way, go ahead. Millions of people do. In the end they will be sorry, but by then it will be too late to do anything about it.

"So what will it be, men? The way of the cross or the way of the world? You've got to invest your life somewhere. What's the best deal you can make?"

THE KNOCK AT THE DOOR

Perhaps a contemporary illustration will help us understand the challenge Jesus gave to His disciples. Not long after the fall of the

Soviet Union, I had the privilege of eating supper with a pastor from St. Petersburg, Russia. During the evening he told us what it was like to grow up in a Communist country. His father (a pastor for over forty years) used to tell his mother, "Some night we may be sleeping when suddenly there will come a knock at the door. When that happens, don't be surprised if the KGB takes me away in the middle of the night and you never see me again. When that happens, don't give up the faith. After I am gone, remember that the Lord will never leave you."

During the Communist years many Christians were taken to the prison camps and psychiatric hospitals and made to suffer horribly simply because of their faith. Some believers spent twenty-five years or more behind bars for the sake of the Gospel. A few of them came out and wrote books about their experiences. But most of those who suffered for God did not write any books because they did not want any publicity. They viewed their time in prison as part of their ministry for God. Their attitude was, "If God can use me more effectively in the Gulag, then that's where I will serve Him."

After seventy years of oppression, the people of Russia are just now getting used to freedom. Many western Christians are bothered by one question: why would God allow the Communists to oppress the people for seventy years? There are many negative answers to that question; but around the dinner table that night, the pastor offered a positive answer that went something like this:

> After all that has happened to us, the church in Russia is almost like the first-century apostolic church. We have nothing but a pure faith in God. Our churches are not corrupted by many things that corrupt churches in the West. I believe that a great revival is coming to the world in the last days, and I believe that the Russian church will send out thousands of missionaries around the world. In order for us to be ready for that, we had to be oppressed by the Communists.

That is part of what it means to "lose your life" for Jesus' sake. Though it may cost you dearly in terms of this world's goods, in the end you will accomplish far more than if you had taken the easy road.

WAS JESUS A FAILURE?

What is the best deal you can make? The life of Jesus is the best answer to that question. Consider the facts of His "career":

- He was born in an obscure village in an out-of-the-way province of the Roman Empire.
- He never went to college, nor did He have any professional training.
- He never had a bank account.
- He owned no property except the clothes on His back.
- He never held public office.
- He never wrote a book.
- He never had a wife or children.
- His closest friends were blue-collar workers.
- He felt at home among the outcasts of society.
- His ministry consisted of preaching in the countryside, teaching in the synagogues, answering difficult questions, healing the sick, and casting out demons.
- His opponents openly accused him of consorting with the devil.
- Along the way, He made many powerful enemies by exposing corruption in high places.
- Finally, His adversaries captured him, tried Him in a kangaroo court, and put Him to death.

To be perfectly honest, by most modern standards we would consider Him a failure. He never made it to the top. If ever a man seemed to waste His life, it was Jesus.

But consider this. After 2,000 years . . .

- His words are remembered and repeated around the world.
- His followers number in the hundreds of millions and can be found in every country on earth.
- His personal integrity stands unsullied amidst the attacks of the cynics and the sneers of the ignorant.

- His death, which seemed to be a tragedy, has become the means by which we can be reconciled to God.

- His whole mission on earth, which seemed to be a failure, has now become history's greatest success story.

How can this be? He was humiliated to the point of death and seemed to lose His life for no purpose whatsoever. And yet through His death God exalted Him to the very highest position in the universe, "that at the name of Jesus every knee should bow" and "every tongue confess that Jesus Christ is Lord, to the glory of God the Father" (Philippians 2:9-10).

Jesus made clear why He did what He did when He said, "Unless a kernel of wheat falls to the ground and dies, it remains only a single seed. But if it dies, it produces many seeds" (John 12:24). Out of one seed comes forth a vast harvest; but that seed must die in order to bring forth fruit. As long as the seed "saves" its life, it remains alone. But when it "loses" its life, it brings forth the harvest.

It's simple, really. If you try to "save" your life, in the end you "lose" it. But if you dare to "lose" it for Jesus' sake, in the end you "save" it. Jesus himself is the supreme example of this principle.

CAREER VS. MISSION

There is yet another way of looking at this whole question of "losing" and "saving" your life. Let me do it by asking this question: *is your life a career or a mission?*

There is a vast difference between those two concepts. A quick glance at a dictionary reveals the essence of the difference:

- A career is something *you choose* for yourself.

- A mission is something *chosen for you* by someone else.

For the sake of convenience, we can display many of the differences this way:

CAREER	MISSION
Chosen by you	Chosen by God
Do something	Be something
Your goals for your life	God's goals for your life

"I can do it"	"Bigger than me"
"I want it all right now"	"I'm willing to wait for God"
Ladder to climb	Journey to take
Present satisfaction	Future fulfillment
Horizontal focus	Vertical focus
Tangible rewards	Intangible rewards
Happiness	Joy
Destination primary	Journey primary
"My career is my life"	"My mission is my life"
"I am a professional"	"I am a disciple"
Make a mark	Do God's will
Make it to the top	Take up the cross
"My kingdom come"	"Thy kingdom come"
Build a fortune	Lay up treasures in heaven
Focus: Performance	Focus: Relationship with God
Market-driven	Holiness-driven
Image-conscious	God-conscious

There is a huge difference between living for your career and being sent on a mission. The Bible never talks about having a career. Having a career is *not* a biblical issue. Having a mission is.

IS THAT ALL THERE IS?

It is not that believers don't have careers. We do. Some of us are painters, some are doctors, some are computer scientists, some are bankers, some are nurses, some are teachers, and some are writers. Some are homemakers and mothers (an honorable and often-overlooked career). But the difference is this: *the people of the world live for their careers; the people of God don't.*

When your career is the most important factor in your life, then you are career-driven and career-minded while you climb the career ladder. You take a job and leave it two years later because it's a "good career move." You break all the significant relationships in one place and move across the country because your career demands it. Everything is calculated to get you some-day to that elusive place called "The Top." When you get there, your career will be complete, and the world will applaud your achievements.

I am suggesting that being career-minded in this sense is pre-cisely what Jesus meant when He said, "Whoever wants to save his life will lose it." Your career may well keep you from fulfilling your mission in life; and your mission may never make much sense as a career.

- Your career is the answer to the question, "What do I do for a living?"

- Your mission is the answer to the question, "What am I doing with my life?"

If you are just here to eat, sleep, go to college, get a degree, get married, get a job, have some children, climb the corporate lad-der, make some money, buy a summer home, retire gracefully, grow old, and die . . . then what's the big deal? All of that is okay; but if that's all there is to life, you are really no different from pagans who don't even believe in God.

Let's put it this way: Jesus calls His followers to be totally sold out to His kingdom. That applies to *all* Christians *all* the time, not just to "full-time Christian workers" such as pastors or mission-aries. Suppose you are an electrical engineer or an attorney. Here is God's job description for you:

- You are a missionary cleverly disguised as an engineer.

- You are a missionary cleverly disguised as an attorney.

It's nice to have a career; it's far better to be on a mission for God.

It's not wrong to have a career and do well by the world's stan-dards. Nor is it sinful to move across the country. I've already shared the story of my good friend who is moving away from Chicago because he is truly attempting to follow God's will for his life. But motivation is everything. Two people may follow the same career path, and both may end up at the top. Yet one may be living solely for his career, while the other sees his life as a divinely ordained mission from God. One has "lost" his life; the other has "saved" it, just as Jesus said.

Ask yourself, did Jesus have a career? No; He had a mission from God to be the Savior of the world. Nothing He did makes sense from a career point of view. Being crucified is not a good career move. Yet by His death He reconciled the world to God. Was He a success or a failure?

A MAN WITH A MISSION

So I slapped my hand on the table and said to my friend, "I know exactly what God wants you to do. He wants you to go back to Texas, get back into that Ph.D. program, get your degree, and go make a difference in the criminal justice system of America. Do you understand the position you're in? We all agree that the criminal justice system is corrupt in America, and we all agree it needs reforming. But how? And who will do it?

"I can't do it. I'm just a layman when it comes to criminal justice. I can say all I want, but the professionals won't listen to me. I don't know anything about the ins and outs of criminal justice. Everything I know I get by watching *Perry Mason* reruns. I have no influence whatsoever.

"We need men and women who believe the Bible, who are trained at the very highest level in criminal justice, who are willing to pay the price in time and sacrifice to get the degree from the best schools in America, who unashamedly bring their evangelical faith into the classroom and attempt—however imperfectly—to proclaim the Lordship of Jesus Christ over our criminal justice system. Where can we find such men and women?

"They would have to be born-again Christians. They would have to be trained in the Bible. They would have to be unafraid to speak out. They would have to go through the most rigorous training. They would have to pay the price up-front in order to make an impact later.

"We truly need men and women like that in order to make an impact on the criminal justice system in America. Where will we find them? You fit all those criteria. And you are about to quit the program. Don't quit. You can make a difference for the kingdom of God within the criminal justice system.

"We can always get more Christian cops, but where will we get enough highly-trained people ready to speak out for God to the criminal justice system? Stay in school and get your degree."

He looked startled, and then a grin slowly spread across his face. "Pastor, I never thought about it like that. I guess I was just thinking about getting my degree and going to teach somewhere. I never thought about it as a mission from God."

Then I said, "If you are just going to get your degree so you can teach somewhere, forget it. We've got enough professors already. If getting your Ph.D. is just a career move, forget it. It's not worth the sacrifice. But if you believe God has called you to make a difference for him within the criminal justice system, then you need that Ph.D. in order to speak to the system with total credibility. It all depends on whether you want a career or a mission."

A BRAND-NEW COMPUTER

My friend returned to Texas, and I wondered what he would do. About a month later he wrote me a letter saying that he had decided to go ahead and complete the program. And he added an interesting footnote.

Once he decided to finish the program, he knew he needed to go ahead and buy a computer. So he shopped around and found what he thought was a good deal. One Sunday while attending church he happened to mention his plans to buy a computer. A man hearing his story said, "Give me the details and I'll have one of my people check it out for you." My friend gave the man the details about the system he proposed to buy, and the man gave it to one of his employees.

A few days later the man came back and said, "This isn't the best deal. Here is what you really need . . ." The hardware and the software the man proposed cost several hundred dollars more than the system my friend already couldn't afford.

Before my friend could say anything, the man said, "My wife

and I have decided we would like to buy this computer system for you as our investment in your life."

That's what happens when you stop looking at your life as a career and start viewing it as a mission. People catch the vision and rally to your support.

THE REST OF THE STORY, SO FAR

Two years later my friend earned his Ph.D. Although he was contacted by several prestigious universities, he turned them down in favor of a professorship at a lesser-known school. Why? Because he is on a "mission from God." It's really that simple. He believes that if God wants him at a better-known university in a few years, the Lord will make that plain. In the meantime, as a brand-new criminal justice professor, he now has an unlimited opportunity to discuss the problem of crime and its cure—Jesus Christ. He started a new campus ministry, serves as the faculty adviser for Campus Crusade for Christ, and served as the point man for bringing the "Back to Genesis" seminar to the main basketball arena on campus where several hundred students were exposed to the truth about God the Creator.

He recently wrote me with good news about more open doors for sharing Christ on his campus. At the same time, God continues to prosper his career. Neither he nor I can say with certainty what the next few years will hold for him. But I do believe that my friend serves as an excellent example of what the Lord can do through a life that is truly surrendered to Him.

THE GREATEST MISSION ON EARTH

As we wrap up this chapter, let me suggest several implications of the truth about "losing your life" for Christ. First, *we need to challenge our teenagers to see themselves as being on a mission for God.* Too many times we talk as if "having a career" is what life is all about. But why bother staying pure if your ultimate purpose in life is to get an education so you can start a career and build a fortune? Where is the motive for saying no to temptation? Our only hope is to challenge the next generation to "lose their lives" for Jesus' sake. Then and only then will they have the spiritual resources to stand up against the incoming tidal wave of evil. Why lose your life in pursuit of an MBA just so you can retire to Florida in forty-five years? Big deal. Life ought to add up to something more than that.

Let's start challenging our children to a standard far higher than the empty call of materialism. Let's tell them about the only thing that really matters in life—following Jesus in the greatest mission on earth.

Second, *every Christian needs to do a career/mission inventory from time to time.* Too often we agonize over God's will because we have a career orientation instead of a mission orientation. So we make our decisions strictly from a worldly basis regarding money, position, influence, titles, salary, benefits, staying on the right career path, backing the right people, and so on. But Jesus has already warned us that you can have all those things and still lose your own soul. Following Christ is the way to life!

The question is not, what are you doing for a living? The deeper issue is, What are you doing with your life? Why did God put you here on the earth?

A quick illustration may help. A friend took me out to lunch recently to share what God is doing in his life. My friend served for about ten years as an international business consultant. Along the way he worked with several multinational corporations in England, Brazil, and Italy. Right now he is "in transition," beginning his own consulting firm in the Midwest. In talking about what it meant to be a Christian in the business world, my friend made a comment that stuck in my mind: "If you are happy and productive in your current job, the only reason to take a promotion is to leverage your position for the kingdom of God."

That's a tremendous insight. Use the bigger position to impact the world for Jesus Christ. Don't just climb the ladder in order to get to the top. Realize that God has put you where you are "for such a time as this." Understand that behind every open door and every promotion stands the Lord God who rules heaven and earth. As you climb to the top, remember who put you there.

Too many Christians routinely make wrong decisions because they are too career-minded and not mission-focused. What a huge difference it makes to see all of life as belonging to the Lord Jesus Christ!

THE ANSWER MAKES ALL THE DIFFERENCE

The martyred missionary Jim Elliot said, "He is no fool who gives what he cannot keep to gain what he cannot lose."

If you try to save your life, you'll lose it in the end. If you lose your life for Jesus' sake, in the end you will save it.

If you live for your career, what difference will it make ten seconds after you die? If you spend your life in the service of the kingdom of God, the road may not be easy, but 10,000 years from now you'll never regret your decision.

Do you have a career, or are you on a mission for God? The answer to that question makes all the difference in the world.

QUESTIONS FOR PERSONAL/GROUP STUDY

1. Most people agree that getting a good education is absolutely vital. But how much education is enough? In the major story of this chapter, the man eventually got his Ph.D. Few of us will go that far. What biblical principles should guide our decisions regarding how much education we need?

2. When should career issues enter into the picture? How do we factor in the "mission for God" principle?

3. Across the centuries some skeptics have mocked Jesus as a misguided rabbi whose life was a dismal failure. What evidence could you muster to support such a charge? How would you refute it? In your opinion, what was the "mission" of Jesus Christ? Did He succeed or fail? Explain your answer.

4. Name three ways we can instill a "mission for God" orientation among our teenagers.

5. Since all of us will have a career of one kind or another, how can we ensure that our career is part of our mission in life? Could two people have the same career and perhaps even work side-by-side, and yet one is on a mission for God and the other is simply climbing the career ladder? How would the difference between the two be seen in daily life?

6. Read Mark 8:34-38 carefully. Now imagine that Jesus is speaking to you personally. Paraphrase His words as you would imagine He would say them if the two of you were talking together. How do these words apply to your interests, hobbies, career aspirations, and relationships?

GOING DEEPER

Have you discovered your mission in life? Not your career, but the basic reason God put you on this earth. How does your life stack up against the career vs. mission comparison in this chapter? Set aside ten minutes a day for the next week to think and pray about God's mission for your life. Factor in your natural talents, your spiritual gifts, the major events (both good and bad) of your life, and your answer to the question, "What is God's purpose for my life?" Then write a one-sentence mission statement. Write it down, and place the statement where you can see it every day. Memorize it, and share it with at least one other person. You may be surprised to see your life taking on a new, more purposeful direction.

CHAPTER FIVE

The Hardest Prayer You Will Ever Pray

Some prayers are harder to pray than others. I learned that years ago when my father died. One October day he felt a pain in his shoulder. The doctors later said it was transferred pain from a bacterial infection elsewhere in his body. It did not seem serious at first, but he got no better and a few days later traveled by ambulance to Birmingham where a battery of doctors went to work on him. Marlene and I drove in from Dallas, arriving at the hospital sometime after midnight. Dad spoke to me when I saw him, but I could tell he was desperately ill.

A few days later, now back in Dallas, we received the dreaded call. Once again we sped through the night to Birmingham, hoping against hope. But my untrained eyes told me that he was not long for this world. That day—it is etched forever in my mind—I went in to see him, and he did not know me. He was drugged and nearly in a coma. Leaning against the wall outside the Intensive Care Unit I wept furious tears, unable to keep back the truth—my dad was dying and I could do nothing about it.

I must have prayed that day. I'm sure I did. After all, I was in seminary learning to help other people draw near to God. But I didn't pray with words. In that terrible moment of utter helplessness, prayer did not come naturally. All theology aside, I knew my father was dying. I could hardly pray, "O God, heal him," for I

77

knew in my soul that God was not going to answer that prayer. I could not pray, "O God, take him home and end the pain," for he was my father and much too young to die. I prayed, "O God," but that's about all. In a few days, God mercifully intervened and ended my father's ordeal.

PRAYING IN THE DARKNESS

Most people have been in the same place. You have stood beside the bed of a loved one and found that prayer was nearly impossible. Or you have faced a difficulty so immense that you truly did not know what words to use when you prayed. Or perhaps there have been times in your life when you have not prayed because you were afraid of the answer God would give.

Prayer can do that to even the best of us. It seems easy on Sunday morning. Why is it so difficult to pray in the darkness? Perhaps we are afraid of what God will say in response to our prayers. What if we ask for guidance and He guides us in ways we don't want to follow? What if we pray for wisdom and the wisdom we receive seems more like nonsense? What if we pray for patience and the answer means nothing but trouble for us?

A LITTLE MORE LIKE THE ANGELS

All of this should not surprise us. Jesus hinted at the problem when He gave us the Lord's Prayer. Included in that model prayer were these words: "Your will be done on earth as it is in heaven" (Matthew 6:10). The basic difficulty may be easily seen if we lay it out in a series of logical statements:

1. God has a will concerning my life.
2. God's will encompasses His desires for my life.
3. But I also have a will that encompasses my desires for my life.
4. Those two wills are often in conflict with each other.
5. When there is a conflict, either God's will or my will will prevail.
6. When I pray, "Your will be done," I am asking for God's will to prevail over my will.

That's the basic difficulty we face when we pray. *When we ask that God's will be done, we are implicitly asking that our wills be over-*

turned, if necessary. It's not easy to pray that way when you're standing beside the hospital bed of someone you love.

But that's only part of the problem. Jesus taught us to pray that God's will might be done "on earth as it is in heaven." Exactly how is God's will being done in heaven? If the reference is to the angels (as I think it is), then God's will is *always* being done in heaven. Psalm 103:20 says, "Praise the Lord, you his angels, you mighty ones who do his bidding, who obey his word." In heaven, God's will is *always* done; in heaven, God's will is *instantaneously* done; in heaven, God's will is *completely* done; in heaven, God's will is *joyfully* done. In essence, Jesus asks us to pray that we might become a little more like the angels (who always obey) and a little less like the demons (who never obey). When that happens, the earth will become a little more like heaven and a little less like hell.

But God's will is rarely done on the earth. After all, there are over five billion wills on the earth and still only one will in heaven. Just look around you. Do you see God's will being done? Pick up the newspaper and read about a serial killer. Read about the killing in Bosnia, the slaughter in Rwanda, the corruption in high places in America, the rise of satanic ritual child abuse. It looks like someone else's will is being done.

In some ways, "Your will be done" seems like the most hopeless of all prayer requests. Seldom do we mean it. Seldom does it seem to be answered.

"Your will be done" is a difficult prayer to pray sincerely. It may be the hardest prayer you will ever pray. Even though Jesus Himself instructed us to use these words, there are at least four reasons why we find it difficult to do so.

REASON #1:
It is hard to pray, "Your will be done" because it means giving up control of your own life

We're back to that little syllogism again:

1. God has a will (or desire) for your life.
2. But you also have a will (or desire) for your life.
3. When you pray, "Your will be done," you are asking that His will take precedence over yours.

Only one will can be done at a time. Either God calls the shots or you call the shots. Either He is in control or you are in control. It's not easy to pray like that because it means giving up control of your own life.

But you aren't really in control anyway. It only seems that way.

PROVERBS 20:24

Recently I helped officiate in a wedding ceremony for two students attending a local Christian college. During the rehearsal I had a nice talk with a professor from that college, who was also taking part in the ceremony. In the course of our conversation he brought up a verse I had never considered before—Proverbs 20:24, "A man's steps are directed by the LORD. How then can anyone understand his own way?" That didn't seem remarkable until the professor mentioned that the word for "man" in the first part of the verse is not the usual Hebrew word. It is another Hebrew word that means "a mighty warrior." The Old Testament writers used that particular word to speak of great soldiers who marched valiantly into battle. These were the "mighty men" of Israel who possessed great strength and courage.

We could legitimately translate the first part of the verse this way: "Even the steps of a mighty man are directed by the Lord." Think of the "mighty men" of this decade. Their names are Schwarzkopf, Powell, Bush, Clinton, Gorbachev, Yeltsin, Arafat, and, in another category, Jordan, Shaq, Nicholson, Schwarzenegger, and Stallone.

They appear to be self-made men, self-sufficient, able to run their own lives. But it only appears that way. Solomon says that behind the power and image of the mighty man stands the Lord Himself. He is the one who directs their paths.

That brings us to the second half of the verse: "How then can anyone understand his own way?" The word translated "anyone" is actually the normal Hebrew word for "man." In this context, it has the idea of "mere mortal man." If even the mighty man cannot direct his own steps, how then can any of us be sure about the future? If the people we look up to are at the mercy of higher hands, then how can any of us claim to fully understand the direction of our lives? The answer is, we can't. The mighty man can't. The average man can't. You can't. I can't. No one can.

DAVE DRAVECKY

Consider Dave Dravecky. In the late 1980s he was one of the rising stars of professional baseball. He pitched for the San Diego Padres and later for the San Francisco Giants. His future seemed bright as he won game after game with a blazing fastball and a mean curve that dipped and dropped as it passed over home plate. Then it happened. A strange soreness in his left arm. An examination. A biopsy. Cancer. Just like that, his career seemed in jeopardy. Surgery was followed by months of rehabilitation. Then a stint in the minor leagues. Then his great comeback game. Five days later he pitched in Montreal. No one who has seen the video will ever forget it. He threw a pitch, and his weakened bone snapped. This time there would be no coming back.

Several months later the doctors removed his left arm and a large part of his left shoulder. It was the only way to rid his body of cancer once and for all. After the surgery he issued a brief statement thanking his many friends and fans for their love and prayers. He said he looked forward to a life free from pain.

A "TEMPORARY SETBACK"

There was no further word until he spoke at a convention in Orlando. His words were reported by newspapers and TV stations around the country. To Dave Dravecky, his amputation was just a "temporary setback." He said he plans to swim and play golf and tennis now that he is no longer playing baseball. He also planned to continue speaking around the country.

At a time when many people would be drowning in self-pity, Dave Dravecky was looking to the future. "There is no struggle about feeling sorry for myself. The question is not, 'Why me, God?' The question is, 'What is Your plan for me?'" Then he answered his own question: "I see this as God giving me the opportunity to share the Gospel with a lot of people."

There are many positive lessons that might be drawn from his example. For our purposes I will point out just one: no one, not even a mighty man like Dave Dravecky, directs his own path. Surely he would not have chosen the path the Lord chose for him. Who would "choose" to have cancer and lose an arm? But Dave Dravecky's path was "directed" by the Lord. It is entirely to his credit that he understands that fact and publicly glorifies God in a circumstance that would have embittered many other people.

"EVERY DAY I PRAY, 'THY WILL BE DONE'"

I'm thinking of another man right now—not as well-known as Dave Dravecky—but a "mighty man" in his own right. For many years he has been rising to the top of his profession. I do not know his salary, but I am sure he is well-compensated for his labors.

This week we ate lunch together. His outward prosperity is only part of the story. In his life he has known more than his share of pain and sorrow. Tragedy struck close to home once and then twice. He is outgoing and friendly, and you feel drawn to him immediately; but if you look closely at his eyes, there is heaviness there. He bears burdens about which only his close friends know.

Right now he's in the middle of great turmoil in the place where he works. The details don't matter. But every day he faces the reality of going to work knowing that his superiors have not appreciated his contributions to the firm. It's a real battle to get up, go to work, and keep a smile on his face.

But he looked so relaxed when I ate lunch with him. How does he do it? A great change has come across his life in the last few days. It's a change on the inside, a change in the way he looks at things. "Pastor, I've been pushing and pushing and pushing. Trying to fix things up. Trying to make a better deal. Holding all my cards, dealing them out one by one. It hasn't worked. The Lord finally said to me, 'Why don't you let Me take over?' So I did. I told the Lord He could take over. Nothing has changed at the office. Things are going to get worse before they get better. They're going to make things miserable for me. But that doesn't matter. I've given it all to the Lord. That means I don't have to figure out all the details of my future." Then he said, "I'm going to relax now."

He's a good man in a hard place. But you wouldn't know it to look at him. Somehow he has grasped the great truth that praying, "Your will be done" means letting go of your own life. My friend has learned it the same way we all have to learn it—through hard experience.

As we were walking back to his car, he said, "Every day I pray this simple prayer, 'Thy will be done.'" No wonder he has a smile on his face.

It's hard to pray that prayer because it means giving up control of your life. But that doesn't mean your life will go out of control. It just means that your life is surrendered to God's control.

REASON #2:
It is hard to pray, "Your will be done" because we often doubt that God wants the best for us

There is a second reason why this is a difficult prayer to pray. If the first one touches our will, the second one touches our mind. The first reason was practical; the second is theological. Oftentimes we're scared that if we give God control of our lives, He'll mess it up somehow. We wouldn't say it that way, but that's how we really feel.

More than once I have heard people say, "Pray for the opposite of what you want, because God always gives us the opposite of what we ask for." We laugh when we read that because it seems so absurd. But many of us secretly wonder if it isn't true. We've all known the frustration of unanswered prayer. Perhaps it was for something small—like a new dress for a Saturday night date. Perhaps it was for God to give you a basset hound. Perhaps you asked God to open the door for you to go to a certain college. Or perhaps it was for something truly big—prayer requested at the bedside of a loved one, prayer for a wayward child, prayer for a failing marriage. When God doesn't answer our prayers—or when He doesn't answer in the way we want Him to—are we not tempted to wonder if God gives us the opposite of what we ask for?

DOES GOD KNOW MY NAME?

Our biggest problem is not, "is there a God?"—because virtually everyone agrees that the answer is yes. Even people who never come to church and people who consider themselves irreligious would answer yes. The much greater question is, "is there a God in heaven who cares about me?" Millions of people—including millions of apparently loyal churchgoers—secretly wonder if the answer to that question might be no. A God who is there—yes. A God who cares for me—maybe not.

Perhaps some wonder if this does not reveal a kind of spiritual schizophrenia. How can you answer yes to one question and no or maybe not to the other? Is this not some kind of internal contradiction? If there is a God, surely He cares about me. And if He doesn't care for me, who cares whether there's a God or not?

But those questions reside on two different levels. The existence of God is primarily a mental or logical problem. It's an issue of philosophy. The question concerning God's personal concern is entirely different. Very often it is asked by those who have known deep pain and suffering. For them the question is very personal: "if God cares for me, how could He let my son die?" Or, "where was God when my husband lost his job?" Or, "why didn't God keep that man from shooting my father?" These are not abstract questions about first causes and the argument from design. These are questions wrenched from the depths of horrible despair.

How do you pray, "Your will be done" when you aren't sure that God really cares for you? If you knew—really knew—that He had your best interests at heart, you might dare to pray that way. But as long as you doubt, that prayer will be almost impossible.

HE BOWED HIS HEAD AND DIED

There are many answers to the question, "does God really care for me?" But there is only one that really matters. It's the answer God gave 2,000 years ago on a hill outside the city walls of Jerusalem. On a hot Friday afternoon the Romans crucified a man they thought to be a Jewish rabble-rouser. Only later did they understand who He really was. His name was Jesus. He came from a small town in Galilee called Nazareth. He started His ministry by preaching in the synagogues. As He went from village to village, His fame spread, until thousands came out to hear Him. At length the powers-that-be found Him to be a threat to them, and they decided to eliminate Him. It took a long time to trap Him, but they finally arrested Him with the help of a traitor from His inner circle.

Once arrested, He was tried, beaten, mocked, insulted, cursed, abused, slapped, scourged, and crowned with thorns. Eventually He was condemned to die. For six hours He hung on a cross—naked before the world, exposed to the elements, reviled by the crowd, jeered by His enemies, mourned by those who loved Him. At the end, after suffering excruciating pain, He bowed his head and died.

HIS NAME IS FATHER

After all that, God says, "Do you still wonder if I love you?"

For some people, even the death of God's Son will not be enough. But if that is not enough, nothing God can do will make any difference. For if someone will give His own Son to die, is there anything else He will hold back? Money is nothing compared to a son.

That's why the most crucial word of the Lord's Prayer is in the very first phrase—"Our *Father* in heaven." To call God *Father* means that you recognize what He did when He gave His own Son to die on the cross. "Father" is not some phrase to toss around when we pray. It's what Christian prayer is all about. God is worthy to be called "Father" precisely because He has done what good fathers must do—He has sacrificed the best that He had for the welfare of His children.

Look to the cross, my doubting friend. Gaze on the Son of God. Ponder the meaning of Golgotha. Who is that crucified on Calvary's tree? His name is Jesus. Study His face. See the wounds in His hands, His feet, His side. Was it not for you that He died? Do you still doubt that God loves you?

That's the second reason why this prayer is difficult. Many of us doubt that God truly cares for us. The third reason moves us into a completely different arena.

REASON #3:
It is hard to pray, "Your will be done" because God's will sometimes involves suffering and pain

That was true for Jesus. The scene has shifted to Thursday night. It is late—perhaps 10:30 or 11:00 P.M. The Lord now retreats to His favorite spot—the olive groves in Gethsemane. Leaving Peter, James, and John behind, He wrestles in prayer with what is about to happen. He knows with the perfect knowledge of omniscience that the time has come for Him to die. All is revealed; nothing is hidden. It was for this moment that He came into the world. Nothing will surprise Him—not Judas' wicked kiss, not Caiaphas' mocking words, not Pilate's curious questions. The pain, the blood, the anguish—all of it is as clear to Him as if it had already happened.

Most of all He sees the darkness. Sin like a menacing cloud hovers over Him. *Sin!* The very word is repugnant to Him. Sin in all its ugliness, all its vile reaches, all its putrefying force, now looms before Him. It is as if a giant sewer is being opened, and the foul contents are flooding over Him. All the evil that men can do, all the filth of uncounted atrocities, the swill of the human race, the total iniquity of every man and woman from the beginning of time!

As Jesus sees the cup filled with human scum approaching him, He recoils in horror. These are his words: "My Father, if it is possible, may this cup be taken from me. Yet not as I will, but as you will" (Matthew 26:39).

These are not the words of unbelief. They are words of faith. They are the words of a man who understands fully what it will cost to do the will of God.

Was it wrong for Jesus to pray this way? Did it somehow reveal a lack of trust in God? I think not. No one was ever more committed to doing the will of God. He did not pray because He wished to be released from the will of God. He prayed because He knew how much the will of God would cost Him personally. He was willing to pay the price, but in the horror of seeing the "cup" of suffering draw near, He asked that it might be removed from Him.

If Jesus in His extremity struggled with the will of God, should we be surprised if we do the same? If it was difficult for Jesus to pray, "Your will be done," is it likely to be any easier for us?

Jesus is Exhibit A of what it costs to pray, "Your will be done." It cost Him his life. No wonder He struggled in Gethsemane.

THE UNDERGROUND CHURCH

Several years ago *Reader's Digest* carried a lead article entitled "China's Daring Underground of Faith" (August 1991, pp. 33-38). It told the story of Pastor Lin Xiangao, one of the leaders of the underground church movement in China. When the Communists took over in 1949, most Christian workers fled the country. Pastor Lin was offered a safe parish in Hong Kong but turned it down, preferring to stay in Canton with his own people. Already there were rumors of mass executions, but Pastor Lin stayed because "I felt it was my duty to suffer for the Lord."

The knock on his door came in 1955. He was jailed for sixteen months, released, jailed again, and held in various labor camps until 1978. Soon after getting out, he resumed his ministry, building a congregation of hundreds of people. Now we will fast-forward to 1990:

> Following an evening service on February 22, 1990, policemen burst into Lin's tiny house. They confiscated all the Bibles and hand-stenciled tracts, along with hymnals, tapes and recorders, an organ, and a mimeograph machine. They also seized his membership lists.
>
> Government officials warned Lin's followers not to attend his services, and he was ordered to stop preaching. For a time he complied. But he struggled inwardly and finally felt called to preach again. As he resumed his ministry, the police summoned him for numerous interrogations. To all demands Lin replied quietly, "I have spent twenty years in your prisons. I fear nothing anymore" (p. 35).

The writer of the article ends his story this way:

> As I left Lin Xiangao's home, I asked him if he thought he would be jailed again. "Perhaps," he replied. "But we are Christians and difficulty brings us closer to Christ." He paused for a moment and then added simply, "Pray for us" (p. 38).

Don't let that last phrase slip by you. "We are Christians and difficulty brings us closer to Christ." Here is a brother who understands what it means to pray, "Your will be done." He knows how hard it is, but he has prayed the prayer anyway.

"Your will be done" *is* a hard prayer to pray. Jesus knew it. Pastor Lin knows it. Blessed are those who know it and pray the prayer anyway.

REASON #4:
It is hard to pray, "Your will be done" because you are praying against the status quo

God's will is seldom done on the earth. Too many things that go on are obviously not God's will. Abortion . . . crack babies . . . broken homes . . . rampant pornography . . . men starving, women freezing, children wearing rags . . . racial prejudice . . . ethnic hatred . . . serial killers on the loose . . . corruption in high places.

Sometimes it seems as if God has gone to sleep and Satan has taken over. Now ponder the next sentence carefully: *God does not accept the status quo.* He does not accept Satan's usurpation of His rightful place in the world. He does not accept that sin should reign forever on the earth. He does not accept that the killing should go on forever. God does not sit idly by while the world goes to hell.

God does not accept the status quo!

In fact, He sent His own Son into the world to change the status quo. What the prophets couldn't accomplish with their words, His Son accomplished by the Incarnation. At Bethlehem God sent a message to the world: "Things are going to change."

If things were okay, why did God send His Son? But things weren't okay. They were wrong, dreadfully wrong, and getting worse all the time. So God intervened in human history in the most dramatic fashion possible.

NO SAINTLY RESIGNATION

To pray, "Your will be done" is to follow God in opposing the status quo. This prayer goes against the grain. In a world where God's will is *not* done, we are to pray that God's will *will* be done.

Those are fighting words, words that rebel against everything that is evil and wrong on Planet Earth.

All too often when we pray, "Your will be done," we do it with an air of pious resignation: "O God, since I am helpless to stem the tide of events, may Your will be done." Sometimes we use it as an excuse not to get angry at the sin and suffering all around us. But if God does not accept the status quo, neither should we!

Let me say it plainly: to pray, "Your will be done" is an act of God-ordained rebellion! This is not a prayer for the weak or the timid. This is a prayer for troublemakers and rabble-rousers. It is a prayer for believers who look at the devastation all around them and who say, "I'm angry, and I'm not going to take this lying down."

It is a prayer, then, that leads necessarily to action. If you see injustice being done, you cannot blithely pray, "Your will be done" and then walk away. If you really mean, "Your will be done," you've got to jump into the fray and help make it happen.

YOU'LL NEVER KNOW UNTIL YOU LET GO

Let me summarize everything I've said in this chapter: "Your will be done" is hard to pray. There are at least four reasons:

1. It is hard because it means you have to give up control of your own life.
2. It is hard because many of us doubt that God truly cares for us.
3. It is hard because God's will may involve pain and suffering.
4. It is hard because God's will is so often not done in this world.

Every point is true. And yet Jesus told us to pray this way.

It's not wrong to struggle with this prayer. After all, Jesus struggled with it Himself. But over the years I've discovered that the happiest people are those who have said, "I've decided to let go and let God run my life." So many of us go through life with a clenched fist, trying to control the uncontrollable, trying to mastermind all the circumstances, trying to make our plans work. So we hold tightly to the things we value—our career, our reputation, our happiness, our health, our children, our education, our wealth, our possessions, even our mates. We even hold tightly to life itself. But those things we hold so tightly never really belonged to us in the first place. They always belonged to God. He loaned them to us, and when the time comes He will take them back again.

Happy are those people who hold lightly the things they value greatly. The happiest people I know are those who have said, "All right, Lord, I'm letting go. I'm going to relax now and let You take over."

What are you struggling with right now? What are you holding on to so tightly that it almost makes your hands hurt? What is it that you are afraid to give to God? Whatever it is, you'll be a lot happier when you finally say, "Your will be done" and open your clenched fist. But you'll never know until you let go.

C. S. Lewis said there are two kinds of people in the world, and only two kinds: those who say to God, "Your will be done" and those to whom God says in the end, "Your will be done." Which kind are you?

A SIMPLE PRAYER

Here's a simple prayer that may help you loosen your grip on the things with which you are struggling:

> *O Lord, Your will be done—*
> *nothing more,*
> *nothing less,*
> *nothing else.*
> *Amen.*

As always, we who pray that prayer are called by God to be part of the answer. We are to pray, "Your will be done," and then we are to see that God's will *is* done in our own lives.

> *Your will be done . . .*
> *in my life*
> *in my family*
> *in my finances*
> *in my career*
> *in my children*
> *in my dreams for the future*

in my words
in my friendships
in my world.

When we pray that way, God will always be pleased to answer us. The answer may not be what we want or what we expect, but the answer *will* come, and we will not regret having asked. And best of all, when we pray that way, we are doing our little part to make the earth a little more like heaven and a little less like hell.

QUESTIONS FOR PERSONAL/GROUP STUDY

1. Have you ever faced a moment so desperate that you felt you couldn't pray? Can you think of a time when you were afraid to pray, "Your will be done" because you feared God's answer? Describe your experience and God's response.

2. True or False: God's will is rarely done on the earth. Explain your answer.

3. Why do you think God chose Dave Dravecky to go through such an ordeal? What does his example say to you?

4. Did Jesus lack confidence in God when He prayed in Gethsemane? If the answer is no, then what is the meaning of "If it be Your will, let this cup pass from Me"?

5. How do you feel about the statement, "God does not accept the status quo"?

5. In what sense is the prayer "Your will be done" an act of God-ordained rebellion against the evil of this world?

6. What happens to the person who refuses to pray, "Your will be done"?

GOING DEEPER

When you pray, "Your will be done," you are asking that your life pass from your control to God's control. Think about the last twenty-four hours. Who has been in charge—you or the Lord? What are the signs that you are trying to control your own life? Circle the words that apply to you: irritable, pushy, anxious, fearful, hyperactive, withdrawn, driven, compulsive, critical, hypersensitive, perfectionistic, overbearing, worried. Spend some time asking God to set you free from the need to always be in control.

CHAPTER SIX

Don't Get Fleeced!

Beginning with this chapter, we are taking a sharp right turn in our quest to discover God's will. Up till now we've surveyed various biblical passages in order to draw out some basic principles. For the next six chapters we are going to look at some of the common problems and questions associated with the will of God.

The first question concerns putting out a fleece. You may have heard of this somewhere along the way even if you don't know what it means. "Putting out a fleece" or "fleecing" (whether or not the term is understood or used) is a common technique for determining God's will.

WHAT IS A FLEECE?

In its most general sense, *putting out a fleece refers to seeking to learn the will of God by means of a predetermined sign.* People generally use a fleece when they come to a point of decision and don't know what to do. Maybe you're faced with a job offer and don't know whether to say yes or no. So you say to God, "Please give me a sign." For instance, "If they offer me a salary that is $20,000 more than my current salary, I'll take that as a sign from God that I should accept the job." In that case, the $20,000 would be the fleece.

You are putting out a fleece when you say, "God, I am asking

You to give me a sign, and this is the sign I want You to give me." It's that second part that really qualifies as putting out a fleece. It's not just asking for guidance. It's when you say, "Lord, I want You to do such-and-such, and if You will do what I have asked, I will know what Your will is."

WHAT IS THE BIBLICAL
BACKGROUND FOR FLEECING?

In order to answer this question, let's travel back in time some 3,300 years to meet a man named Gideon. The angel of the Lord (a special appearance of God) came to him one day and said, "The Lord is with you, mighty warrior" (Judges 6:12). This surprising word came in the midst of the Midianite oppression of Israel. The Midianites were a vast army from the east who invaded Israel riding on camels. They came each year during harvesttime just as the Israelites were reaping their crops. They would plunder the land, get on their camels, ride out of town, and then stay away until the next year's harvest. Then they would come back and do it all over again.

So every year at harvesttime the Jews were losing everything they had worked for because of the Midianites' invasion. The people of God were reduced to living in caves because they were frightened of the mighty power of the Midianites.

In response to this crisis God tapped Gideon on the shoulder and said, "I am going to use you to deliver My people." The angel of the Lord was very clear on that point. "Gideon, you're the man who will deliver My people." He repeated it two or three times in Judges 6. Gideon responded, "Who, me?" "Yes, you." "You've got the wrong man." "No, I don't. You're the man, Gideon."

The following verses detail the various things God did to convince Gideon that he was indeed the right man for the job. First, *Gideon asked for a sign from God so he would know that he was really talking to the angel of the Lord* (v. 18). When Gideon placed his offering on a rock, the angel touched the meat and the bread with the tip of his staff. "Fire flared from the rock, consuming the meat and the bread" (v. 21). Gideon correctly concluded from this supernatural sign that the angelic visitor was genuine. He says as much in verse 22: "Ah, Sovereign Lord! I have seen the angel of the Lord face to face." When God assured him he was not going to die, Gideon built an altar to commemorate the event.

Second, *God directed Gideon to tear down his father's altar to Baal and to build an altar to the Lord.* When Gideon tore down the pagan altar, he and his men did so at night because they were afraid of public reaction (v. 27). As it turned out, his fear was well-founded because the people of Ophrah were ready to put him to death the next morning. But his father intervened, reasoning that Baal could defend himself and didn't need any help from the townspeople.

Third, *when the Midianites prepared for their annual invasion, the Spirit of the Lord came upon Gideon in great power, equipping him to lead the people of God* (v. 34). He sent messengers to Manasseh and the neighboring tribes, calling the men to battle.

All was now set for the showdown between the men of Israel and the invading Midianites. God had found His leader—the reluctant Gideon—and had reaffirmed His call through a miraculous sign, had protected him from a lynch mob, and had filled him with the Holy Spirit. The men were gathered, the enemy was approaching, and everyone was ready for the great battle. Everyone, that is, except Gideon. He was still not sure if he was the right man to lead Israel.

GIDEON KNEW!

Before we look at the story of the fleece, note this fact: *Judges 6 is perfectly clear that Gideon knew exactly what God wanted him to do.* The fleece was simply meant to *confirm* God's will, not to *determine* God's will. He actually said as much in Judges 6:36—"If you will save Israel by my hand *as you have promised.*" Verse 37 says, "Then I will know that you will save Israel by my hand, *as you said*" (italics added). No matter what conclusion you come to about the modern practice of fleecing, remember that originally it was used to *confirm* God's will, not to *determine* it.

Gideon is one of the most fearful men in all the Bible. Although he was a great hero, he was also filled with fear. *In twentieth-century terms, he was a man with low self-esteem.* He didn't feel very good about himself. Gideon doubted that God could use him to deliver Israel.

So in spite of everything else that had happened, he asked God to give him one more confirming sign. Judges 6:36-40 sets the scene for us:

> Gideon said to God, "If you will save Israel by my hand as you have promised—look, I will place a wool fleece on the threshing floor. If there is dew only on the fleece and all the ground is dry, then I will know that you will save Israel by my hand, as you said." And that is what happened. Gideon rose early the next day; he squeezed the fleece and wrung out the dew—a bowlful of water. Then Gideon said to God, "Do not be angry with me. Let me make just one more request. Allow me one more test with the fleece. This time make the fleece dry and the ground covered with dew." That night God did so. Only the fleece was dry; all the ground was covered with dew.

The first time the sheepskin was soaking wet, so much so that Gideon squeezed out a bowlful of water. That makes sense because a sheepskin would draw the moisture out of the air. The only unusual fact was that the ground was bone-dry. That was unusual, but it was not absolutely *impossible*.

Gideon was still not sure; so he timidly asked God to do it again, only backwards—the ground wet and the sheepskin dry. That would be much more unusual because the fleece would normally get wet from the dew. The next morning the ground was wet, and the fleece was bone-dry.

The message is clear. *Gideon received double confirmation of what he already knew to be the will of God.* Judges 7 goes on to tell the amazing story of how God used Gideon in a very unlikely way to win a great battle with the Midianites.

NOT THE SAME

Before we leave this question, let's nail down the central point. *The way most people today use fleecing is not the same way Gideon did.* We use the fleece today when we are uncertain about what God wants us to do. We don't know if we should get married or not; we're not sure if we should send our kids to a public school or a

Christian school; we're torn between two good job offers; we don't know whether to move to the suburbs or stay in the city. We use a fleece when we don't know the will of God. But Gideon already knew God's will.

That's a crucial issue. The fleece was never used to *determine* God's will. The only time that it was ever used was to *confirm* God's will, which had already been made unmistakably clear.

Typically people today use fleecing as a predetermined sign to ascertain God's will. "I'm thinking about buying a new car. I don't know whether I should or not. Lord, if You will send me $500 by tomorrow afternoon, I'll know it's Your will for me to buy a new car."

Or maybe your boss offers you a new job. Should you take it or not? So you say, "Lord, if my boss calls me between 2:00 and 3:00 this afternoon, I will know it is Your will for me to take this job."

Perhaps you are thinking about moving to another city. You have a decision to make. Should you move or not? So you say, "Lord, I'm not sure what You want me to do, but if I wake up tomorrow morning and there are four inches of snow on the ground, I will know it is Your will for me to move."

Let's suppose you are in college and find yourself becoming interested in a young man you see three times a week in your Advanced Ceramic Design class. You are wondering if this is the guy for you. So you say, "Lord, when I see him after class tomorrow, if he smiles at me, that will be a sign that we should get married." That's a fleece. It's a predetermined sign that you use in order to determine God's will. Christians use fleeces all the time when facing major life decisions.

All of which brings us to the second important question.

WHAT KIND OF FAITH DID GIDEON HAVE?

Gideon was a man of very weak faith. Hebrews 11:32 makes it clear that he did have faith. But the record in Judges 6 shows that his faith—though genuine—was weak. In Judges 6:12 the angel of the Lord appears to Gideon and says, "The Lord is with you, mighty warrior." Gideon immediately starts to argue. He sees all the problems and none of the possibilities. "How can I be a mighty warrior? Where is God? Where are all the miracles?"

The angel of the Lord answered, "Go in the strength you have and save Israel out of Midian's hand. Am I not sending you?" (v. 14). Immediately Gideon starts to argue again: "But, Lord, how can I save Israel? My clan is the weakest in Manasseh, and I am the least in my family" (v. 15). The Lord answered, "I will be with you, and you will strike down the Midianites as if they were but one man" (v. 16).

"Not me. You've got the wrong guy. Lord, I think You made a mistake. I come from Manasseh. Nobody great comes from Manasseh. And my family is the weakest of all the families in Manasseh. And I'm the least in my own family."

So Gideon asks the angel to let him bring an offering as a sign that God is going to use him. The offering is immediately consumed with fire (6:17-21). It's an absolute miracle. So Gideon gets the sign he asks for.

We must evaluate the fleece episode against that background. Three times the angel said, "You are the man." Then Gideon asked for and received a miraculous sign that he was the one. After all that, he was *still* unsure. "Lord, I know what You want me to do, but I still have my doubts. I'm insecure. I feel inferior. I don't feel up to the task." When the fleece is wet and the ground is dry, even *that* is not enough. You can hear apology in the words he uses—"Do not be angry with me. Let me make just one more request" (v. 39).

Let me state one fact very clearly. I am not suggesting that what Gideon did was wrong. It was not a sin to ask God for a fleece; but it was a sign of his weak faith because he already knew what God wanted him to do. If you make that a habit or a pattern in your life, it is a sign of weak faith in your life. When you look at Gideon's life, you don't see a man of great robust faith—you see a man of weak faith whom God nevertheless used greatly.

WHAT DOES THE NEW TESTAMENT SAY ABOUT FLEECING?

The answer is, nothing at all. However, that's a significant point. *There are no examples in the New Testament where anyone ever put out a fleece in order to determine God's will—or even to confirm it.* And you only find it once in the Old Testament. You never read any passage where the Apostle Paul advises the believers at Rome or Philippi or Ephesus to put out a fleece to determine God's will. There are no examples of anything like that in the New Testament.

Casting Lots

Some people have found a parallel in the story of the eleven apostles casting lots in Acts 1 to find a replacement for Judas. They nominated two men—Joseph and Matthias. They then cast lots, and the lot fell to Matthias; so he was added to the eleven apostles. First of all, this not a parallel because the apostles truly didn't know which man God had chosen. Second, casting lots was an Old Testament practice that is used in Acts 1 as a kind of "holdover" during the transitional period before Pentecost and the birth of the church through the descent of the Holy Spirit. Third, casting lots was a recognized and oft-repeated Old Testament practice, but putting out a fleece happened only once and was never repeated. In light of all that, it's hard to see how Acts 1 parallels Judges 6 in any meaningful way.

Looking for a Sign

In Matthew 12:38-39 the Pharisees asked Jesus for a miraculous sign to prove He was the promised Messiah. "A wicked and adulterous generation asks for a miraculous sign!" Jesus replied. Please meditate on that carefully. *Demanding miraculous signs from God is not necessarily a sign of strong faith.* It is often a sign of a very weak and immature faith. In this case it was a cover for an unbelieving heart. Jesus repeats His words in Matthew 16:1-4. When the Jewish leaders come asking for a sign from heaven, Jesus says, "A wicked and adulterous generation looks for a miraculous sign, but none will be given it except the sign of Jonah." The sign of the prophet Jonah is a reference to Christ's coming resurrection from the dead. He is saying, "I've already told you everything you need to know about what God can do. Why do you come asking Me for something extra?"

DOUBTING THOMAS

Then we have the case of Thomas—the man who would not believe in the resurrection of Christ until he put his hands into the wounded side of Jesus. Jesus didn't humiliate him or belittle his lack of faith. "He said to Thomas, 'Put your finger here; see my hands. Reach out your hand and put it in my side. Stop doubting and believe'" (John 20:27). Jesus met him at the point of his weakness. But what did Jesus say next? "Because you have seen me, you have believed; blessed are those who have not seen and yet have believed" (20:29).

There is one level of the Christian life that says, "Lord, You've got to show me first. I've got to see a sign before I will believe." There is another level that says, "Lord, You said it. I don't see any signs. But I believe what You said." It's better to say, "Lord, I'm going to do Your will—signs or no signs, fleece or no fleece."

When you know God's will, you are to do it. Period. End of discussion. It is a weak form of Christianity that says to the Almighty, "You must meet my conditions before I will do Your will." Second Corinthians 5:7 offers the biblical perspective, "We live by faith, not by sight." You can say this another way: "We live by faith, not by fleeces."

WHAT ARE THE DANGERS OF FLEECING?

I'll mention three answers to that question. First, *fleecing often leads to uncertainty and confusion.* What about the man who says, "I'll buy this car if the Lord sends me $500 tomorrow"? What do you do if the next day you get $485? Do you say, "Close enough"? No. You asked God for $500. Does it have to be *exactly* $500, or are we talking ballpark numbers here?

There's no way to answer a question like that with any certainty. Since you made up the "rules," is it okay to "bend" them, or are you then guilty of trying to help God out?

The second danger is that *fleecing comes very close to attempting to manipulate God.* The Bible repeatedly warns us against putting God to the test. What does it mean to put God to the test? *It is any attempt to box him in according to our human understanding.* "Lord, if You are going to work, let me tell You exactly how You have to work in my life."

Let's go back to the example of the person who says, "I'll take the new job if my boss calls me between 2:00 and 3:00 P.M." Fine, but what if your boss calls at 1:30 P.M.? You have boxed

God into a sixty-minute period in your life. And that's a way of putting God to the test.

The third problem is this: *you end up shifting responsibility from yourself to God, thus destroying the need for faith.* That brings us again to a fundamental insight regarding God's will. Generally speaking, it is not God's plan to show you your personal future. More often, God shows you the next step and that's all. Too many times fleecing is an attempt to force God to show you the future.

When I shared this with my congregation, someone said, "Your sermon on fleecing made one thing very clear. You still have to choose." He's right. You still have to take responsibility for your choices. Fleecing is an attempt to shift responsibility for our decisions from us to God, thus destroying the need for faith and responsible decision-making. Too often we want to know the future when God's will is merely to show us the next step we should take.

You still have to choose. After all the prayer, all the Bible study, all the counsel, all the meditation, all the writing down of options, after you've agonized, still the moment comes when you must decide. God won't take the responsibility for you. If you're going to take that new job, you've got to decide for yourself. If you are going to sell your house, you can't wait for God to write a message in the clouds. You've got to sign the papers yourself. God isn't going to do it for you.

Fleecing is an attempt to stand at the fork in the road forever without making a decision. It destroys the need for faith and decisive action. But to put the matter that way leaves out an important perspective.

IS IT ALWAYS WRONG TO ASK FOR A SIGN?

The answer is no. It's not wrong to ask for a sign if you are simply asking for guidance as to the next step you should take. "Father, make Your will plain so I will know the next step." Is that a fleece? No, because you are not boxing God in. You are just asking God to do what He said He would do—to make plain the path you should follow.

But it is boxing God in if you say, "Lord, in order to know the next step, I want my boss to call between 2:00 and 3:00 in the afternoon." That comes close to black magic and superstition. There's a huge difference between asking for guidance and trying to squeeze God into a mold of your own making. We should say, "Lord, I stand on the verge of making a big decision. I need to know the next step I should take. I pray that You will make it clear to me."

Sometimes asking for a sign is nothing more than using sanctified common sense. In Matthew 10:11-16 Jesus advises His disciples on how to discern God's will in certain situations:

> "Whatever town or village you enter, search for some worthy person there and stay at his house until you leave. As you enter the home, give it your greeting. If the home is deserving, let your peace rest on it; if it is not, let your peace return to you. If anyone will not welcome you or listen to your words, shake the dust off your feet when you leave that home or town. I tell you the truth, it will be more bearable for Sodom and Gomorrah on the day of judgment than for that town. I am sending you out like sheep among wolves. Therefore be as shrewd as snakes and as innocent as doves."

Jesus instructs His followers to look for certain outward indicators in order to find God's will. "When you go to a town, if they want to listen, preach to them. If they don't, go someplace else." This is a very simple strategy: if they listen, stay there; if not, go someplace else. Shake the dust off your feet. That's not a fleece. It's using common sense to properly analyze the situation and to draw good conclusions regarding what God wants you to do. That's what I mean by sanctified common sense.

Is it always wrong to ask for a sign? No; not if you are simply asking for guidance and not trying to box God in.

WHAT IS THE ESSENTIAL DIFFERENCE BETWEEN A SIGN AND A FLEECE?

With this question we come directly to the heart of the issue. One essential difference is that *a fleece is an unusual event unrelated to the particular guidance you need.* For instance, finding snow on the ground does not necessarily signal that you should move to Florida. Likewise, seeing clouds shaped like penguins doesn't mean God is calling you to be a missionary to Antarctica. This isn't to say that God couldn't arrange the circumstances of life to cause these things to happen or that He might not use them in your life. But there is no *necessary* connection between the unusual event and the guidance desired.

That brings us back to Judges 6 and Gideon's fleece. The sign was *clear*, it was *unmistakable*, and it was *miraculous*. So what's wrong with that? Nothing, really. Gideon asked for an unrelated sign, and God granted his request. However, the request came from weak faith, and the requested sign had nothing to do with whether or not the Midianites would be defeated. Presumably Gideon could have asked for some other sign, which God could have given him.

For the reasons I've already mentioned, I don't recommend the practice of asking for unrelated, specific signs as a means of determining God's will. It is fraught with too many difficulties and possible misinterpretations.

"THE DEVIL COULD HAVE SENT US $23,500"

However, there are times when asking for a *related* sign may be the course of wisdom. Early in his ministry Billy Graham was considering an offer to begin a nationwide radio ministry. It seemed like a good idea, but where would the funds come from to support such a venture? It would be far worse to start a radio ministry only to see it fail than never to start at all. It happened that the offer came during a crusade in Portland, Oregon. After praying about it, Billy decided to ask God for a sign to indicate if he should go ahead with the idea. Specifically, he asked God to bring in $25,000 by midnight of that same day if God wanted the radio ministry to begin. It's crucial to note at this point that $25,000 was more than just a sign; it represented the initial start-up costs for the ministry. It's also important to know that Graham felt that the radio ministry should be supported by many people—not just a few rich contributors. That's why he decided to ask the crusade audience to support this new idea that *very day*. Thus, the sign requested—and even the timing of it—was directly related to the guidance desired.

After the service that night, people lined up to give money to the new project. When everything was counted, the total came to $23,500. The two men proposing the radio ministry suggested that was close enough. "The devil could give us $23,500," Billy replied. It had to be at least $25,000. The team returned to their hotel feeling somewhat dejected. Shortly before midnight, one of Billy's coworkers went to the hotel desk where he was given three envelopes. When he opened them, he found they contained cash and pledges for exactly $1,500. The "fleece" had been met exactly as Billy Graham had prayed it would a few hours earlier.

My only comment—other than to marvel at God's miraculous provision—is that this isn't exactly parallel to what Gideon did. Gideon knew God's will; Billy Graham didn't. Gideon's sign was unrelated to the guidance needed. The $25,000 was directly related to the expenses necessary to start the *Hour of Decision* radio program. And asking the crusade audience to support this new project *that night* demonstrated the wide support necessary to make the radio ministry successful over the long haul.

Don't miss the larger point here: asking for a sign isn't wrong, especially when the sign is directly related to the guidance you need. But simply asking for a sign from God isn't necessarily "putting out a fleece." It may simply be using sanctified common sense in a given situation. "If the money comes in, we'll start. If not, we won't." I can see nothing wrong with that approach to determining God's will if it is used in conjunction with other indicators such as prayer, searching the Scriptures, and listening to wise counsel.

Let's wrap up this chapter with three concise conclusions regarding fleecing.

CONCLUSION #1:
Fleecing can be dangerous, misleading, and manipulative and can lead to a subjective faith in God

That statement should make my position clear. I've already said that many believers use this method to determine God's will. I've done it myself. *If this is your habitual pattern for finding God's will, stop.* This is not the best way because you are in danger of trying to put God in a box.

If you haven't used this method of finding God's will, don't start, because it can easily lead you to make a foolish decision.

CONCLUSION #2:
Seeking wisdom and putting out a fleece are different

Seeking wisdom simply means asking God for His direction for the next step without boxing Him in. Putting out a fleece is an attempt to limit God in order to discover the future. And that's not valid. God will show you the next step, but He is not committed to showing you the future.

It also helps to remember that seeking wisdom involves looking at relevant circumstances. Saying, "I won't buy that car unless I have $3,000 in the bank" is not asking for a fleece; it's simply a prudent financial decision. But saying, "If it snows on July 4th I'll know God wants me to move to Detroit" is foolish because you are asking for a sign that has no relation to the decision you are making. A fleece involves selecting an arbitrary or unrelated sign that actually attempts to force God's hand by causing Him to reveal the future. Wisdom means asking God for specific guidance involving the relevant circumstances of the decision you need to make. You may need to think about that for a bit, but the distinction is both real and crucial.

CONCLUSION #3:
Mature faith relies less on spectacular signs and more on wisdom from God and sanctified common sense

That sentence more or less sums up this entire chapter. My conclusion is this: is it wrong to put out a fleece? No, it's not wrong. Is it unwise? In my opinion, the answer is yes. Does God guide His children? Yes, He does. Does that mean we have to put out a fleece in order to help Him do it? The answer to that is no.

Our problem is we want to stay at the baby level of Christianity. We want to stay in spiritual diapers so we won't have to take responsibility for our own decisions. That's why we constantly ask for signs, though what we need to do is trust God and then take decisive action.

What is it that God wants from us? Simple faith. No one has ever improved on the words of Solomon: "Trust in the LORD with all your heart and lean not on your own understanding; in all your ways acknowledge him, and he will make your paths straight" (Proverbs 3:5-6). "In all your ways," not "in all your fleeces." There is a difference.

Our Father wants to bring us to the place where our trust is in Him alone, not in circumstances or in fleeces. He wants to bring us to the point where we are willing to move out at His command with signs or without them.

There's a phrase for this: *naked faith*. God wants us to have faith in Him apart from the circumstances, apart from the fleeces, apart from our own scheming and manipulation—nothing but faith in Him alone. *Trust in the Lord with all your heart and—with or without fleeces—He will direct your paths.*

QUESTIONS FOR PERSONAL/GROUP STUDY

1. Probably the most difficult aspect of this chapter is properly defining "fleecing" as it relates to the will of God. Take a few moments to read Judges 6 carefully. How much did Gideon know about God's will before putting out the fleece? Why did he ask for this additional sign?

2. Gideon was a man of weak faith. As you read Judges 6, at what points did he demonstrate faith and at what points did his doubt come through?

3. How would you have responded if you had been in Gideon's situation?

4. Can you think of any times when you were facing a tough decision and you "put out a fleece"? What happened? What lessons did you learn from those experiences? Under what circumstances, if any, would you advise a friend to "put out a fleece"?

5. According to this chapter, the crucial element in "putting out a fleece" is asking for an unrelated sign. List the dangers of this practice.

6. What is the fundamental difference between asking for guidance and putting out a fleece?

GOING DEEPER

Tony just graduated from high school and is trying to decide where to go to college. He has narrowed his choices down to a local community college, a Christian college in another state, and a large university about seventy-five miles from home. After praying about it, he decided to apply to all three colleges, believing that he should attend the first college that accepted him. Letters of acceptance from all three schools arrive on the very same day. Confused, he comes to you for help. How would you advise him to proceed?

CHAPTER SEVEN

He's in Charge—So Relax!

Nothing is more important for the Christian than becoming fully persuaded that God does indeed lead His children on their journey from earth to heaven. If you doubt that fact, you will struggle through life feeling as if every major decision rests solely on your shoulders. What a difference it makes to know with great conviction that behind your life stands the unseen hand of God working in, through, and sometimes in spite of your decisions to accomplish His will in your life. If reading this book does nothing else, I hope it builds your confidence in God.

This very week as you come to that moment when you must decide to go one way or the other, you can have confidence that God (though perhaps unseen and unheard and not traced by the five senses) is leading you in exactly the direction He wants you to go.

Perhaps you've read these famous lines by James Russell Lowell. They describe the Christian view of life in a fallen world where values have been turned upside down:

> *Truth forever on the scaffold,*
> *Wrong forever on the throne.*
> *Yet that scaffold sways the future, and,*
> *   behind the dim unknown*
> *Standeth God within the shadows, keeping*
> *   watch above His own.*

The last line contains the heart of the Christian philosophy of history. God stands "within the shadows, keeping watch above His own." When the world seems most out of control, God steps in to let us know that He keeps watch over us. Often it is only as we look back that we see the hand of God working through the circumstances of life.

With that in mind, let's return to the life of Abraham, to an episode from his final days on earth. Up until this point we have been talking about discovering the will of God in general terms and laying down some helpful principles. Now we are going to study the question of discovering God's will as it applies to one of the central issues of life—the question of marriage. *For most of us— apart from the decision to trust Jesus Christ—there is no bigger or more important decision that we will ever make.*

WHO'S THE LUCKY PERSON?

The question of marriage resolves itself into two sub-questions. The first is, should I get married? The second is, who's going to be the lucky person? Both questions are understandably difficult. Should I get married or should I stay single? Most of us could make a pretty good argument either way. There are always reasons to get married; and as Paul points out in 1 Corinthians 7, there are plenty of good reasons to stay single.

It's important to emphasize that fact as we begin this chapter. The Bible makes it clear that both marriage and singleness are gifts from God. Marriage answers the problem of human loneliness (Genesis 2:18). When Adam met Eve, he found more than a wife—he found a companion, a lover, and a best friend. But marriage—as good as it is—is not for everyone. Singleness can also be a gift from God, as 1 Corinthians 7:7 clearly teaches. In fact, Paul seems to affirm the higher value of singleness because the single person is free from the entanglements of marriage. The single person is free to serve the Lord wholeheartedly (cf. 1 Corinthians 7:32-35). Paul goes so far as to say that those who are single should stay single (vv. 8, 27). Marriage is not a sin (v. 28), but it can distract a man away from undivided service for the Lord (v. 33). Paul concludes with a word to Christian widows (vv. 39-40). They are free to remarry if they wish, but the men they marry must be Christians.

How does this apply to the search for God's will? The answer is, God gives you freedom in this area. Some will choose to stay single, and others will choose to marry, while some will find themselves single at one point in life, married at another point, and for various reasons single again. You are free to choose as you like, with the qualification that believers should not be unequally yoked with unbelievers (2 Corinthians 6:14-18) and that God's instructions regarding divorce and remarriage must be followed (cf. Matthew 5:31-32; 19:1-12; 1 Corinthians 7:10-16).

To state the matter that way raises another question: is God involved at all in the marriage process? Will God lead two Christians to come together at just the right time? Can Christian parents trust the Lord to lead their children to the right marriage partners? If God gives us freedom in this area, does He involve Himself at all in the process of choosing a spouse? I believe the answer is yes. Although not every marriage is made according to God's will, I believe that when Christians truly want to follow the Lord, He will lead them in the choice of a marriage partner.

Genesis 24 is a case in point. It tells the story of the finding of a bride for Isaac. It is the longest chapter in the book of Genesis. It is also the first love story in the Bible. As we examine it together, I would like to offer help in two specific areas. First of all, I think this passage offers some very helpful advice for those who are unmarried and considering the possibility of marriage. Second, this passage reveals some basic biblical principles of God's guidance that apply to all the situations of life. So whether you are single or married, there will be something for you in this chapter.

BACK TO MESOPOTAMIA

In order to understand this passage of Scripture, we have to go back across the centuries to the land of Mesopotamia. This story takes place in a setting that is so strange and so unusual that we can scarcely imagine it.

Yet after you read the story and let its details sink in, it has a very familiar ring. Genesis 24 begins with an anxious father and his unmarried son. The father is concerned about carrying on the family name. He hatches a plan that leads to a prayer, a chance meeting, the watering of some camels, an amazing revelation, a dinnertime speech, a hurried conversation, a crucial question, a decisive answer, a reluctant decision, a long journey, a meeting between a beautiful bride and a bashful husband, a happy wedding, and joy all around.

Though on one level the details are very unfamiliar, on another level there is something here that we can understand. *We all know about love, longing, and loneliness.* We know about waiting for the "right man" or the "right woman." We've all heard about "love at first sight"—even if we've never experienced it.

SOME THINGS NEVER CHANGE

Every year I conduct a number of wedding ceremonies. Not long ago I had the unique privilege of sitting out in the audience instead of performing the ceremony myself. For the first time in several years I got to sit back and relax and enjoy the candles and the music and the singing. There was so much joy and so much happiness. The bride looked radiant in her dazzling white gown, the groom nervous and excited as he watched his beloved come down the aisle. When the minister pronounced the happy couple husband and wife, the audience burst out in spontaneous applause. Afterward several hundred people gathered to celebrate the occasion.

As I thought about it, it occurred to me that although our customs are different, some things are still the same. *Marriage is today what it has always been—two people coming together in the plan of God to live together forever.* In that sense the finding of a bride for Isaac, though an ancient story, sounds amazingly contemporary.

LOOKING TO THE FUTURE

The story of Genesis 24 begins with Abraham. Verse 1 says that he was "old and well advanced in years." As Abraham is coming to his last days, he reflects upon the promises of God, how God had promised him long before that he would have a son. He remembers that through a miraculous conception God had given him Isaac. Now Sarah is dead, and Abraham is soon to join her. God had promised to bring forth a great nation through Abraham, and from that great nation He would bless the whole earth. But in order for the promise to be fulfilled, not only must Abraham have a son, but the son must necessarily be married, and out of the marriage must come children. So Abraham, as he approaches the end of his life, calls his servant and says, "I want you to go find a bride for Isaac."

DON'T MARRY A CANAANITE!

He gave the servant two very specific instructions. Number 1, "You must find a bride for Isaac who does not come from the Canaanites." Number 2, "The bride you find must come from our people."

As Abraham looked to the future, he knew that his son needed a godly wife. *He needed a woman who had been raised among the people of God.* So he said to his servant, "I want you to go back to the land of our relatives." That meant traveling 500 miles across the desert to a place called Nahor. Abraham had learned that a branch of his family still lived there, including a marriageable girl whose name was Rebekah. With his great faith looking to the future, believing that God would guide his servant, he said, "I am sending you to find a bride for my son."

"WHAT IF SHE WON'T COME?"

Immediately the servant thinks about it and asks a very practical question: "What if the woman is unwilling to come back with me to this land?" (Genesis 24:5). Good question. "Shall I then take your son back to the country you came from?" he asks. Abraham answers in verse 8, "If the woman is unwilling to come back with you . . ." *"The"* woman; that is, Abraham believed that God was going to lead the servant to *the* woman. ". . . then you will be released from this oath of mine. Only do not take my son back there."

This leads us to a crucial principle for discovering the will of God: *stay flexible in the light of changing circumstances.* Abraham believed it was the will of God for his son to be married, and he believed that by sending his servant to search for a wife, he was actually doing the will of God. But the servant had raised a very legitimate question. "What if I find *the* woman and she won't come back? What do I do then?" And Abraham says, "Well, don't worry about it. If she won't come, then it's not your problem. Just come on back. We'll decide what to do next."

TROUBLE, TROUBLE, TROUBLE

Many times we start a new project believing that what we are doing is the will of God, and yet very often things do not work out as we planned. You took the job, and it didn't work out. You made the investment, and it didn't work out. You entered the relationship, and it didn't work out. You started school, and it didn't work out. You made a big decision, and it didn't work out. What do you do then? Our first reaction is usually to say, "Well, I must have been wrong; it couldn't have been the will of God."

I don't think that's the right answer.

Trouble does not necessarily mean you are out of God's will. It might mean you are doing exactly what God wants you to do. Sometimes God sends trouble not as a judgment but as a sign that you are doing right. When Jesus was crucified, was He out of God's will? No. Yet His life ended in the midst of pain and suffering. No one was ever more in God's will than Jesus, but He was murdered by His enemies.

The fact that your life hasn't worked out exactly like you planned doesn't necessarily mean your decisions were wrong. Sometimes there are other factors at work.

THE WOMAN, THE WATER, THE CAMELS

So the servant set out on the long journey northeast to Nahor. We are told in verse 10 that the servant took ten of his master's camels and left. It might have taken him a month or so to get there. Eventually he arrived on the outskirts of Nahor in the evening, just about the time the women of the village come out to the well to get water for the camels.

What's his first step? How will he know which girl is the right one for Isaac? Should he conduct interviews, ask them to complete an application, or what? His next step is all-important. He stops and asks God to give him specific guidance.

This is a crucial point. *He asks for specific, direct, unmistakable guidance from God.* He even tells the Lord how he wants it to happen. "May it be that when I say to a girl, 'Please let down your jar that I may have a drink,' and she says, 'Drink, and I'll water your camels too'—let her be the one you have chosen for your servant Isaac. By this I will know that you have shown kindness to my master" (Genesis 24:14)

"LORD, GIVE ME A PURE GIRL TO DATE"

Something like that happened to me twenty-three years ago. During my college days one of my roommates dated several different girls. I didn't pay much attention until he began dating a lovely Christian girl. Eventually they fell in love and were married several years later. Together they raised up a wonderful family to the glory of God.

I remember that when he began dating the girl who became his wife, I said to him, "How did you do that?" He told me how it happened. "Ray, I got tired of just dating one girl after another. One night I knelt down by my bed and prayed, 'God, give me a pure girl to date.' The Lord answered my prayers. I've been dating Anna ever since."

That sounded good to me. So that night when I was by myself, I knelt down and began to pray. "It worked for him—it might work for me," I thought. I prayed the same prayer: "Lord, give me a pure girl to date." I wasn't dating anyone at the time and didn't have anyone in mind. It was just an experiment. I prayed the prayer and promptly forgot all about it.

About three or four weeks later I began to notice this beautiful, sweet, attractive, capable, competent, very intriguing young lady that I had somehow never seen around the campus before. She had been there long before I got there, but somehow in God's providence, at exactly the right moment, I began to notice her. I realized here was a wonderful girl who, frankly, was probably far too good for me. I would be lucky if she ever looked my way.

One Monday night I came back to the campus after leading a youth Bible club and entered the gymnasium at halftime of a basketball game. Looking up in the stands, I saw her—and next to her, a row of empty seats. Turning on the charm, I said, "Do you mind if I join you?" "No," she said with a smile.

The rest is history. We recently celebrated our twentieth anniversary.

It wasn't until I started to date Marlene seriously that I looked back and remembered the prayer I'd prayed that night in my dorm. It hit me that God had precisely and exactly and specifically answered my prayer. From that moment until this, I have never doubted that I am the luckiest man in the world because God gave me a wife in direct answer to my prayer. It worked for my roommate, and it worked for me.

"LET ME WATER YOUR CAMELS"

It also worked for Abraham's servant. As the women approached the well with their water pots, he prayed, "Lord, show me which one You have chosen." Verse 15 tells us that "before he finished praying, Rebekah came out with her jar on her shoulder." He didn't even get the prayer out of his mouth and God was already answering him. Isaiah 65:24 says, "Before they call I will answer; while they are still speaking I will hear." Before the servant finished praying, here came the young ladies, and Rebekah was leading the way!

He still didn't know if she was the one, but she was the first one to the well, and so he said, "Would you give me a drink?" She gladly gave him a drink and then offered to water his camels.

That's *exactly* what the servant had asked for! He prayed, and God answered precisely, down to the tiniest detail.

Here's an important background fact that will shed light on this passage. Camels drink a lot of water. These ten camels had traveled 500 miles from the Negev all the way up to Nahor. Scholars tell us that a camel at the end of a day might well drink twenty to thirty gallons of water. So Rebekah was volunteering to take a bucket and draw 200 to 300 gallons of water!

THE PROOF IS IN THE WATER POT

That leads to a crucial question: *why did the servant ask for this particular sign?* After all, presumably he could have asked for any sign he wanted. Why specify the watering of the camels? First, it was specific and thus easy to determine whether or not it had happened. Second, it was appropriate in that his camels actually needed water. Third, it was an excellent test to discover the kind of woman who would make a good wife for Isaac. After all, his wife was going to become the mother of a great nation. Not only must she be kind and courteous and hospitable—she also must be generous, gracious, industrious, and willing to bear her share of the load. So this wasn't just a frivolous sign or an unrelated fleece. It was a sign that fit the need of the moment.

One quick note: the servant still didn't know if Rebekah was the one. He thought she was, the early signs were encouraging, the answer had come exactly as he'd asked, but he needed confirmation. He still didn't know if she was willing to return with him to meet Isaac.

FIVE HUNDRED MILES

I pause here to note that this is exactly how we discover God's will. *One answered prayer doesn't mean we see the big picture.* Although Rebekah seemed like the right girl, the final determination would come later. All the servant knew was that he must take the next step, trusting God to lead him on. Will Rebekah be the one? It was too early to say for certain.

Nevertheless, the servant stopped to give thanks to God for His remarkable leading so far. "Then the man bowed down and worshiped the Lord, saying, 'Praise be to the LORD, the God of my master Abraham, who has not abandoned his kindness and faithfulness to my master'" (Genesis 24:26-27a). His first thought was for the Lord. His second thought was for his master. His third thought was for himself: "As for me, the LORD has led me on the journey" (Genesis 24:27b). He is saying, "Lord, I praise You because when I was 500 miles from here, You led me straight to Rebekah here in Nahor. You knew exactly how to lead me from where I was to where she was so I could meet the person who would be a proper bride for Isaac."

It's a fantastic thing to know that you are doing what God wants you to do. Did the servant know what was going to happen when he left Abraham's house? Did he plan in advance to meet Rebekah at the well? Did he know he was going to ask for the sign of the watering of the camels? No, no, and no. He knew none of those things. In fact, he didn't know for sure that he would find the right girl or that she would be willing to return with him even if he did find her. *The only thing he knew was that God would guide his steps one by one across the desert sands so that at precisely the right moment he would be exactly where God wanted him to be.*

CLOSING THE DEAL

The rest of the chapter tells how Rebekah introduced him to her brother Laban and her father Bethuel. In typical Middle Eastern fashion, they all gathered for a great evening meal. But before the meal was served, the servant stood up and made a speech. In it he rehearsed for the family how God had led him from the Negev to Nahor. He also told them how rich Abraham was and how Isaac was going to be the heir to his father's fortune. He mentioned Isaac's miraculous conception and repeated Abraham's specific instructions that Isaac's wife must come from among his own people. Finally, he revealed the prayer he'd prayed at the well and God's amazing, immediate answer. Every sentence revealed his great faith in the God who had led him to Rebekah. Verse 49 is the clincher: "Now if you will show kindness and faithfulness to my master, tell me; and if not, tell me, so I may know which way to turn." Like any good salesman, he presses for a decision.

Laban and Bethuel really couldn't say anything when they heard what the servant said. "This is from the LORD; we can say nothing to you one way or the other" (Genesis 24:50). And so they gave their consent: "Here is Rebekah; take her and go, and let her become the wife of your master's son, as the LORD has directed" (Genesis 24:51).

"WILL YOU GO WITH THIS MAN?"

So they gave their consent—somewhat grudgingly, it seems, but they gave it. Then there was the touchy question of how soon she was to leave with the servant for the trip back to meet Isaac. Understandably, her family didn't want her to leave immediately. "But her brother and her mother replied, 'Let the girl remain with us ten days or so; then you may go.' But he said to them, 'Do not detain me, now that the Lord has granted success to my journey. Send me on my way so I may go to my master'" (Genesis 24:55-56). There was a bit of a disagreement; so they decided to let Rebekah decide for herself. "Then they said, 'Let's call the girl and ask her about it.' So they called Rebekah and asked her, 'Will you go with this man?'" (Genesis 24:57-58).

Consider the implications of this question. Rebekah had never met Isaac. She was not being asked, "Will you go with Isaac?" She was being asked, "Will you go with the servant?" That meant leaving her family permanently because she probably would never make the journey back to Nahor again. She had met the servant only twelve or fifteen hours earlier. So on the basis of one evening and the next morning, she was being asked to make a decision that would cut her off from her family for the rest of her life, to go across the desert to a place she'd never seen, and to marry a man she'd never met. "Will you go with this man?" Most of us would say no. But of course, since God was leading, she said yes.

So they made the long journey back to Beersheba. When they arrived, Isaac was working in the fields. As soon as Rebekah saw him in the distance, she jumped off the camel and veiled her face. Then the servant introduced Isaac to his new bride. Isaac did not really know her at all. But he immediately agreed to the marriage. He took her into Sarah's tent—a sign that she was taking Sarah's place in the family. The story ends with these words: "So she became his wife, and he loved her; and Isaac was comforted after his mother's death" (Genesis 24:67).

The overriding truth from Genesis 24 is that the choice of a bride for Isaac was God's choice. He was the One working behind the scenes. He never spoke. He never said anything. And yet clearly the whole point of Genesis 24 is to say that the search was not just a human search, but that behind the affairs of man stood Almighty God. He was the One who led the servant step by step, and the servant was in touch with God so that when he found the right woman and brought her back home, he knew it would be successful because God had made the choice Himself.

> *Abraham sought it.*
> *His servant found it.*
> *The sign confirmed it.*
> *Laban recognized it.*
> *Rebekah accepted it.*
> *Isaac enjoyed it.*

But God is the one who did the choosing. He was the divine matchmaker who orchestrated the details so that the right man and the right woman would come together at precisely the right moment.

"DO YOU BELIEVE IN MIRACLES?"

Only one question remains: does God still work this way today? Can you trust God to do the same thing for you that He did for Isaac and Rebekah? Does God still lead the right man and the right woman together just as He did 3,800 years ago? Can He do it even when our past attempts in this area have ended in failure?

I believe the answer is yes. About a year ago I performed the wedding ceremony for two friends of mine, Tom and Karen Hawkins. I first met Tom about four years earlier. I had known Karen for less than a year, but I actually knew her quite well because she served as our church secretary.

It was my joy to watch her relationship with Tom unfold as the months passed. A few days before they got married, I asked both of them to write down their thoughts, which I later incorporated into the ceremony. Karen spoke about the pain from a past marriage and how she'd learned to live in fear many years ago. But she also quoted 2 Timothy 1:7, "God did not give us a spirit of timidity, but a spirit of power, of love and of self-discipline." She spoke about Satan's attempt to drag her back into the quagmire of the past: "Jesus knows what's best, not me. I also knew I didn't want a man in my life again. Now look at me! I have some dried roses Tom gave me early in our relationship that I use to remind me that the Lord is in charge, not me."

Tom added his own eloquent words:

> Do you believe in miracles? Not just something surprising but real miracles? Three years ago I was able to do little else but get drunk. I was afraid of my own shadow. Every waking moment was consumed with alcohol.
>
> I saw the peace that some Christians had and I longed for that. When I was ready, I became willing to give up all that I was for all He is. Goodbye Tom, Hello Jesus. My life works in a way that I never dreamed possible.
>
> What blows me away the most is that God loved me when I was at my worst. He loved and accepted me right where I was. And He loved me too much to leave me in that condition. He brought me out of despair with lightning speed.
>
> Today I have a beautiful wife and a wonderful son to love for a lifetime.
>
> Do you believe in miracles? I do.

Can God orchestrate the circumstances of life to bring the right people together at just the right time? Will He do today what He did for Isaac and Rebekah? Will He bless His children who turn to Him by leading them to godly husbands and wives? Will He do it even when the past has not been perfect? You don't have to take my word for it. Just ask Tom and Karen Hawkins and many others.

One final word: does Genesis 24 apply to every marriage regardless of the circumstances? The answer is no. Not every marriage is God's will—not even every marriage between two Christians. Wrong motives, sinful behavior, and emotional immaturity often lead people to marry when they should stay single. And sometimes individuals marry the wrong people or for the wrong reasons. Those cases do not parallel the search to find a bride for Isaac.

In this chapter I have suggested that God can and does bring men and women together in His perfect timing. When Christians truly desire to do God's will, they should expect God to lead them in the practical affairs of life, including the choice of a marriage partner. I also think our children need to know this story. By bringing God into the process of courtship, dating, and marriage, we can give them added motivation toward moral purity. This story ought to encourage our children not to rush into marriage in a surge of emotional attraction, but to wait for God's plan to unfold step by step.

LESSONS REGARDING MARRIAGE

This extraordinary story teaches us many important lessons regarding marriage. Let's take a look at three of them.

The best way to prepare for marriage is to become the best person you can be right now

If you study Rebekah carefully, you can find at least six positive traits in her life. She was *kind*. She was *industrious*. She was *godly*. She was *resourceful*. She was *pure*. She was *decisive*.

If you are interested in being married, then do what Rebekah did. *Cultivate those qualities in your life that will make you a better person.* Those same qualities will also make you a better marriage partner.

If you are interested in being married, focus less on future marriage and more on present faithfulness

What was Rebekah doing when the servant found her? *She was simply doing her job.* She was going out to do the very frustrating, hot, discouraging duty of drawing water at the end of the day. She was doing her chores. She wasn't thinking to herself, "Well, maybe tonight I am going to meet the man of my dreams." She wasn't even focused on future marriage. She was focused on present faithfulness.

And that's a great principle for anybody who wants to be married. Don't focus on marriage. *Focus on doing the will of God faithfully where you are right now.*

Remember, if God wants you to be married, He will bring the right person into your life at the right time—you don't have to worry about it

It's been my observation that those people who fret most over being married end up being the least likely people to get married.

Nobody wants to marry someone who is fearful of not being married. This is not a call for laziness, unconcern, or disinterest in dating. It simply means that if you truly believe your life is in God's hands, you can put your dreams of marriage in His hands too and leave them there.

THREE LESSONS REGARDING GUIDANCE

This story also teaches us some universal principles about discovering God's will. Three in particular deserve special mention.

Knowing God's will involves forethought, planning, preparation, and prayer

Did Abraham do the will of God? Absolutely. He saw the need, conceived a plan, called his servant, told him what to do, and even gave his servant Plan B instructions. *Abraham understood the will of God and then took practical steps to see that it was fulfilled.*

Sometimes we get too mystical about God's will. We want dreams and visions and odd things to happen to us. God doesn't always work that way. More often God works through forethought, planning, preparation, and prayer. As you use the ordinary means at your disposal, God takes those means and works through circumstances to see that His will is done in your life. That may include some remarkable events that seem quite miraculous to us. But whether or not we see the miraculous, our responsibility is to use the information we have to make wise plans for the future.

When you are faithful, God will guide you

God holds Himself responsible to guide your life. *When you put Him first, He says, "I will make sure you get to the right place at the right time."* When you focus on God, He takes responsibility for the details of your life.

Obsessive concern over questions like "Should I get married?" lead you down the wrong trail. *Focus on God.* Focus on being faithful to Him and knowing Him. Focus on doing what God wants you to do. He will take care of the details of your life. He did it for Isaac, and He will do it for you.

Since God is in control of the minute details of life,
you can relax, knowing that He will reveal His plan
for your life step by step

God's will is more like a sunrise than a sunburst. Early in the morning the sun begins to peek above the eastern horizon. At first the sky lightens, then the first rays streak across the sky, then the rim of the sun begins to rise slowly from the earth. Eventually the whole sun is revealed, rising until it dominates the sky, giving light to the earth and driving away the darkness.

God's will is like that. At first we see His plan dimly, and then the outline begins to emerge. Slowly, over time, the clouds vanish, the darkness disappears, and the brightness of His presence fills our lives.

Do you get anxious at sunrise because all you can see is the tiny rim of the sun? No, because you know that if you wait long enough you will see the sun in all its brilliance. The same is true of God's plan for your life. You never see everything in advance; but if you wait long enough, God always reveals His will.

So relax! God is in charge. Soon enough the darkness will vanish, and all that is vague will be made perfectly clear.

QUESTIONS FOR PERSONAL/GROUP STUDY

1. If you are married, what was your greatest fear regarding marriage during your days as a single person? If you are single now, what issues do you struggle with as you contemplate the possibility of marriage?

2. In your opinion, what are the four most important qualities to look for in a potential husband or wife?

3. What role does prayer play in finding the right person to marry? What kinds of things should you pray for?

4. If you truly believe that your spouse is God's choice for you, what implications does that have for your efforts to improve your marriage?

5. How do you feel about the way Rebekah suddenly left her family to go with Isaac's servant? Could God ever lead a person to do something like that today? Could you ever see yourself doing something like that?

6. There are four principal characters in this story: Abraham, the servant, Rebekah, and Isaac. How did each person demonstrate faith in God? How did each person discover God's will?

GOING DEEPER

All her life Michelle has dreamed about getting married and raising a family. At the age of thirty-five she fears that she will never meet the right man. Because she is a Christian, she has prayed repeatedly for God to allow her to marry a man who shares her faith in Christ. Although she has had several dating relationships over the years, nothing serious has ever developed. At one point she considered joining a Christian dating service in order to meet eligible bachelors. Discouraged about her prospects and feeling that time is running out, Michelle comes to you for counsel. What do you say to her?

QUESTIONS FOR PERSONAL/GROUP STUDY

1. If you are married, what was your greatest fear regarding marriage during your dating days as a single person? If you are single now, what issues do you struggle with as you contemplate the possibility of marriage?

2. In your opinion, what are the four most important qualities to look for in a potential husband or wife?

3. What role does prayer play in finding the right person to marry? What kinds of things should you pray for?

4. If you truly believe that your spouse is God's choice for you, what implications does that have for your efforts to improve your marriage?

5. How do you feel about the way Rebekah suddenly left her family to go with Isaac's servant? Could (and ever lead a person to do something like this today)? Could you ever see yourself doing something like that?

6. There are four principal characters in this story: Abraham, the servant, Rebekah, and Isaac. How did each person demonstrate faith in God? How did each person discover God's will?

GOING DEEPER

All her life Michelle has dreamed about getting married and raising a family. At the age of thirty-five years that fears that she will never meet the right man. Because she is a Christian, she has prayed repeatedly for God to allow her to marry a man who shares her faith in Christ. Although she has had several dating relationships over the years, nothing serious has ever developed. At one point she considered joining a Christian dating service in order to meet eligible bachelors. Discouraged about her prospects and feeling that time is running out, Michelle comes to you for counsel. What do you say to her?

CHAPTER EIGHT

The School of Suffering

Kevin and Vicki McCullough never planned to adopt a child. When they joined a team from our church on a missions trip to Haiti, Kevin planned to lead a basketball camp, and Vicki prepared to lead a Bible school. But God had other plans. On our first day in Haiti, children from a nearby orphanage came out to meet us. Rosemond and Roseminda were brother and sister, eight and seven years old respectively. Both suffered from years of malnutrition and neglect. But their eyes sparkled with excitement. I'm not sure how it happened, but in the strange alchemy of the heart, those two orphans "adopted" Kevin and Vicki. Before leaving Haiti, the couple began to wonder, "What would it take to adopt Rosemond and Roseminda and bring them to America?" The answer was, it would take a lot. In the best of circumstances, adoption is expensive and time-consuming. Add in the complicating factors of an international, cross-cultural, trans-racial adoption, and it becomes extremely difficult indeed.

Back in America, Kevin and Vicki prayed a simple prayer: "God, if this is Your will, we'll just keep walking through the next door and the next one until You shut one of them." As the months rolled on, Kevin and Vicki found themselves alternating between encouragement and deep despair. Every time they cleared one legal hurdle, another stared them in the face. Meanwhile, the political situation in Haiti continued to deteriorate, making it hard to find the right officials (or sometimes any officials at all) to sign the necessary papers to move the process along. With the help of friends and family members, they raised the several thousand dollars needed to make the trip to Haiti to pick up the children, all the while wondering if things would hold together long enough for the adoption to take place. Every day brought worse news regarding a possible United States invasion. If that happened, all bets were off, because no one could say with certainty how long the American troops would be there or whether the children in the orphanage would be safe.

As the days drew near for the adoption to take place, Kevin and Vicki moved out of their small apartment into their first home. They set aside one room for Rosemond and another for Roseminda. They still needed a few miracles to take place, but in their minds God had already answered so many prayers that it seemed as if the children were already theirs.

SUDDEN DEATH

Then the phone call came. Roseminda had suddenly died. Evidently she had picked up a parasite (a common occurrence in Haiti), had been admitted to a local hospital (which was excellent by Haitian standards), had been treated with the appropriate antibiotics, and seemed to be getting better. On Sunday she was fine. On Tuesday she seemed to be definitely better. Sometime on Wednesday she took a turn for the worse. In the pre-dawn hours Thursday morning, Roseminda died. She was buried that afternoon.

When I got the call, I couldn't believe it. Surely there had been some mistake. What happened? The details were sketchy, but evidently Roseminda's little body was so weakened by years of malnutrition that even with the help of the medicine it couldn't fight off the effects of the parasite.

When Kevin called me, his voice broke into deep sobs. "Why? Pastor Ray, tell me why. Why did this happen when we were trying to do the will of God? We did everything we thought God wanted us to do. Why would He let this happen?"

I did not have an answer that night. The question still hangs in the air weeks and months later: "Why did this happen when we were trying to do God's will?" All I know is that sometimes when we try our best to follow God's plan, the path of obedience leads us through the dark valley of suffering and pain. No one is exempt—not the good or the godly, not the spiritual or the saintly. Every Christian spends some time in that dark valley and most of us come back for a return visit sooner or later.

FOUR WAYS OF DEALING WITH SUFFERING

There are at least four methods that people use when they're facing suffering and difficulty. Each one of these offers a defense against the upheavals of life, but only one is ultimately satisfying.

Denial

This is where most of us begin when dealing with suffering. It's the *John Wayne mentality*. Grit your teeth; smile even when you're hurting; never let them see you sweat. When someone is in denial, they won't admit the truth even when they know you know the truth. You'll say, "How are you doing?" They'll answer, "Great! I'm doing great!" You know they're not telling the truth, and they know you know, but they say it anyway. We're all like that occasionally. There's something in all of us that makes us pretend that everything is OK even when it's not. We pretend the problem is not there, or we pretend that it's not as bad as it really is. After all, the show must go on. Sometimes it's easier to live in the make-believe world of denial than to deal with the harsh reality of pain and suffering.

Anger

Sometimes we react to difficulty by getting bitter at those who have hurt us, and sometimes even by shaking our fists at God. When you don't deal with your anger constructively, it affects every relationship in life—including your relationship with God. *It is impossible to go through life angry at others and still maintain a warm and positive relationship with God.* You can't hate your neighbor and love God at the same time (see 1 John 4:20). Some believers live that way for years—and then they wonder why God seems so distant and their prayers so empty and their Christian experience so lifeless.

I have a good friend who told me an interesting story. She said that she and her husband had agreed to fast together for two days because they were facing a major decision and needed God's guidance. The day before, her mother had called, and they had gotten into an argument. Angry words sailed along the phone lines, foolish things were spoken on both sides, and after it was over she said to herself, "Why do I even bother talking to my mother?"

The next day the fast began, but there seemed to be no answer from the Lord. The following day was Sunday. Early in the morning my friend felt the Holy Spirit prompting her to make things right with her mother. "How could I expect God to guide me when I was so angry?" So before church she called her mom and asked her forgiveness. Later that day the guidance she and her husband were seeking seemed to come down from heaven. They found the peace and mutual agreement that every couple needs when facing a crossroads decision.

Was that a coincidence? Some people might think so. But I believe it is nothing more than the outworking of Proverbs 28:13 in everyday life: "He who conceals his sins does not prosper, but whoever confesses and renounces them finds mercy." Unresolved anger blocks the road of God's blessing. By clogging up the channels of both human and divine communication, such anger does double damage in the human heart.

Blaming Others

This a very popular option. We all use it sooner or later. A man goes through a bitter divorce battle and says, "It's all her fault." Two brothers break up a family business because they don't trust each other anymore. Disgruntled church members blame the pastor because the church isn't growing. The voters blame the President, the President blames Congress, and Congress blames the media. Students blame teachers, parents blame children, wives blame husbands, the Democrats blame the Republicans, the employees blame the boss, and everyone blames the government. It's easier to be a victim nowadays than to accept personal responsibility for your own problems.

Accept It and Learn from It

This is our final option regarding suffering. You can deny it, you can get angry, you can blame someone else, or you can accept what happens to you and begin to learn from it. Of those four choices, only the last one is a truly Christian way of dealing with the difficulties of life. *When trouble comes, you have only two choices. Either you become a victim or you become a student.* How much better it is to be the latter. Being a student means asking yourself, "What have I learned from this? What is God trying to say to me? How can I grow from this painful experience?"

Why talk about suffering in a book about God's will? Two reasons. First, all of us will spend time in the school of suffering sooner or later. In fact, most of us will enroll in more than one course. Second, we need to understand how God uses our suffering to accomplish His will in our lives.

In this chapter I want to look at one of the central passages in the New Testament on the issue of the believer and his suffering. The New Testament contains a number of helpful passages on this subject, but Romans 8:18-27 is one of the most important. This text brings a liberating perspective to the trials of life.

SUFFERING AND GLORY

Verse 18 introduces us to the central idea of the entire passage: "I consider that our present sufferings are not worth comparing with the glory that will be revealed in us." Take a close look at the word "sufferings" and the word "glory." Paul invites us to make a comparison of those two things. Most of us see only our sufferings. We're acutely aware of the bad things that happen to us. But there is another side—the glory side. There are sufferings, and there is glory.

If you could put all the difficulties of your life on one side of the scale, and the glory that will someday be revealed to you on the other side, the glory would be so much heavier that your difficulties would be blown away like a feather. The sufferings of this life, although they are terrible, are not even worth comparing with the greatness of the glory that will be revealed in us. That is a revolutionary perspective on life. If you ever let that thought grip you—that what God has in store for you is far greater than what you are going through right now—it will revolutionize the way you look at your problems.

With that as background, let's consider three unchanging truths. These truths are axioms that form the Christian attitude toward suffering.

TRUTH #1:
Our suffering is temporary

> The creation waits in eager expectation for the sons of God to be revealed. For the creation was subjected to frustration, not by its own choice, but by the will of the one who subjected it, in hope that the creation itself will be liberated from its bondage to decay and brought into the glorious freedom of the children of God. We know that the whole creation has been groaning as in the pains of child-birth right up to the present time (vv. 19-22).

We live in a frustrating world, don't we? Nothing works the way it is supposed to. You buy something, it breaks; you fix it, and it works for a while and then breaks again. Eventually it wears out completely, and you have to replace it. That's what Paul means when he says, "the creation was subjected to frustration." Nothing lasts forever; nothing works right. *We live in a Murphy's Law universe*. Everything that can go wrong, eventually does.

But it's not just creation; it's also you and me. *We don't work right either*. Children are born with horrible defects; we get cancer or Alzheimer's or AIDS or some other wasting disease. If you live long, your body eventually begins to break down, no matter how well you take care of it. That's ahead for all of us, and there is no escape—unless you happen to be in the wrong place at the wrong time and get shot at a freeway rest stop or on the streets of some major city.

MOUNTAINS OF GARBAGE

Verse 21 speaks of "bondage to decay." Every Tuesday morning two trucks come by my house. One picks up the newspapers and the glass bottles for recycling; the other picks up our garbage. The trucks come *every* Tuesday. Why? Because the flow of garbage never ceases. The more we make, the more we spend. The more we spend, the more we use. The more we use, the more we waste. The more we waste, the more garbage we produce. If you doubt that, let the garbage truck drivers go on strike for a week or two. Just see how fast the mountains of garbage pile up all around you!

But frustration is not the end of the story. Verse 21 says that "creation itself will be liberated from its bondage to decay and brought into the glorious freedom of the children of God." The world as we see it is not the world as God created it. Ever since Adam and Eve sinned, all creation has been suffering. That first sin set in motion a process of slow decay. But it won't be that way forever. All creation waits for the day when the children of God will be perfected by the Lord Jesus Christ. The Christian viewpoint on suffering is to say, "Yes, it's bad. But it's not going to last forever. This isn't the last chapter. God has ordained that our suffering is temporary. Something better is on the way."

TRUTH #2:
Our suffering is educational

Not only so, but we ourselves, who have the firstfruits of the Spirit, groan inwardly as we wait eagerly for our adoption as sons, the redemption of our bodies. For in this hope we were saved. But hope that is seen is no hope at all. Who hopes for what he already has? But if we hope for what we do not yet have, we wait for it patiently (vv. 23-25).

We "groan inwardly," Paul says. We groan because of a job we hate. Yesterday a man told me he was going to make a move after fifteen years in the same job. "I can't take it anymore," he said. We groan because of unfulfilled dreams. We groan because our bodies break down. We groan because our marriages break up. We groan because our children go astray. We groan because our friends disappoint us.

Why does God allow such groaning among His children? Why doesn't He do something about it? Doesn't He know what we're going through? Doesn't He care?

Sometimes we begin to question God's character—as if He somehow enjoys seeing His children suffer. We imagine Him looking the other way as we weep. But it is not so. *He knows what we are going through. He cares about our suffering. He feels our pain.*

The Bible says God allows our pain for a purpose. Verses 24–25 tell us that through our suffering God wants to develop two qualities in us:

- Hope
- Patience

Hope is that *settled confidence that looks to the future,* knowing God will someday keep all His promises. Patience is *the ability to endure present hardship* because you have hope in the future.

Our suffering is educational in that it teaches us hope and patience—two qualities that can't be gained any other way. You only hope for that which you do not have. If you have it, you don't have to hope for it. But if you don't have it, then hope teaches you to wait patiently for it.

A MIRACLE BEGINS

Let's return to the story of Kevin and Vicki and the two children from Haiti. The night we learned that Roseminda died, as we wept and prayed together and sought to make sense out of the tragedy, Kevin said, "We have to get Rosemond out of Haiti *now!*" Time was of the essence because in just fifteen days the United States would cut off all airline traffic to Haiti in an attempt to force a change of government. We prayed that night that Rosemond would be in America within three weeks.

One day passed, then another and another. At the memorial service for Roseminda, representatives from the Chicago press came to pay their respects. Their help would prove crucial. The hurdles were formidable. Kevin and Vicki needed a certain document from Haiti in order to meet the requirements of the Illinois state agency overseeing the whole process. Without that document, Immigration and Naturalization would not issue a visa or a passport without which Rosemond could not leave Haiti. Friends gathered to pray; everyone who knew anyone in power called to ask him or her for help. The local NBC affiliate gave the story wide exposure. Meanwhile, the clock was ticking down toward the deadline for the end of all flights from Haiti to

America. Our man in Haiti worked miracles to produce a document signed by three Haitian officials verifying release of custody rights to Kevin and Vicki. But the state agency wouldn't accept it. It had to be issued by a court in Haiti. The very next day he produced a second document signed this time by a judge on Haiti's second-highest court. In order to do that, he had to borrow a friend's car. The friend asked him to fill it up with gas. That meant finding gas on the black market at $20 per gallon.

"GET THIS PLANE IN THE AIR!"

The final hurdle was the issuing of the passport and the physical exam. When they took Rosemond to Port-au-Prince, the person in charge had left the country. That was on Monday. The final flight out was Friday afternoon. The next day the passport was officially issued, and Rosemond was cleared to go to America.

But the drama was not yet over. Kevin and Vicki flew from Chicago to Fort Lauderdale, Florida, on Thursday night. On Friday Kevin was scheduled to fly on the last commercial flight to Haiti. If all went well, he would fly in, pick up Rosemond, and fly out the same day. When he got to the Florida airport, he was told, "Sorry. We're sending only cargo on this flight. We're sending a second plane this afternoon." Later that day the president of the commuter airline discovered that they had no official clearance for the flight. They prayed and called a congressional office in Washington. An aide called the State Department, which gave emergency approval for the flight. The plane took off from Fort Lauderdale at 4:00 P.M. Kevin arrived at the Cap-Haitien airport several hours later, met Rosemond, and prepared for the return flight. Unfortunately, the sun had gone down. That presented a problem since the Cap-Haitien runway had no lights. The Haitian authorities were so impatient to see the plane leave that when the copilot seemed to take too long with his checklist, a soldier put a gun to his head and said, "Get this plane in the air *now!*" Workers drove a pickup truck to one end of the runway and turned on its headlights. The plane took off at 8:15 P.M. They landed in Florida at 11:53 P.M.—seven minutes before the deadline for all incoming flights.

JOY COMES IN THE MORNING

That Sunday when Kevin and Vicki and Rosemond walked down the aisle at Calvary Memorial Church, the entire congregation spontaneously stood and began cheering. The TV cameras were there as Kevin addressed the congregation. He spoke of how difficult the last few weeks had been, how crushed they were by Roseminda's death, how impossible it seemed that Rosemond could get out of Haiti before the deadline. Then he said the words that were later broadcast across Chicago: "This is a message to Oak Park, to Chicago, and to all of America that God is greater."

It had been only two and a half weeks since Roseminda's death, and Rosemond was in America. I thought of those familiar words from the *King James Version* of Psalm 30:5, "Weeping may endure for a night, but joy cometh in the morning."

Our trials teach us many things, not the least of which are patience and hope. Through our tears we learn to wait on the Lord. And in our waiting on God, we discover that the night does not last forever. Eventually the morning sun begins to slip above the horizon, chasing away the darkness and bringing hope for better things to come.

Through suffering God brings us to the place where we must say, "Lord, it's You and You alone." He's teaching us to wait on Him. You may be trying to scheme your way into a better situation. But eventually you'll say, "Lord, if it takes forever, go ahead. Take Your time. My hope is in You."

The last two verses of the passage introduce us to the third axiom regarding the Christian believer and suffering.

TRUTH #3:
Our suffering is beneficial

In the same way, the Spirit helps us in our weakness. We do not know what we ought to pray, but the Spirit himself intercedes for us with groans that words cannot express. And he who searches our hearts knows the mind of the Spirit, because the Spirit intercedes for the saints in accordance with God's will (8:26-27).

It sounds strange to say that our suffering can somehow be beneficial to us. Some would say it even sounds un-Christian. How can cancer be beneficial? How can the loss of a job be beneficial? How can a broken marriage be beneficial? How can public humiliation be beneficial? How can tears at midnight be beneficial?

Our text explains it this way: *our suffering reveals our weakness.* It strips away the mask of self-sufficiency and reveals our utter helplessness. It forces us to confront our own inabilities. It makes us say, "I'm not as strong as I thought I was. I'm not invincible." Our suffering is beneficial when it causes us to come to the end of our self-sufficiency and say, "O God, I can't make it without You."

GOD PRAYING TO GOD!

Verse 26 says that the Spirit *"helps* us in our weakness." The word translated "helps" means "comes to the aid of someone in desperate need." You are in the stands watching a race when you see a runner faltering in the final turn. He stumbles and is about to fall. Seeing that he is not going to make it, you rush from the stands, come to his side, put your arm around him, and say, "Let me help you to the finish line." That's what the Holy Spirit does for us. *He sees when we are in trouble, and He comes to our aid.*

How does He do it? Paul tells us that the Spirit "intercedes for us with groans that words cannot express." The Holy Spirit prays for us. The Spirit (who is himself the third member of the Trinity) prays to the Father (the first member of the Trinity) in the name of the Son (the second member of the Trinity) for us in our moment of weakness. *This is God praying to God on behalf of God's children!* What an amazing thought!

"O GOD!"

Have you ever been in a situation so desperate that you couldn't pray? Have you ever been so emotionally exhausted that you tried to pray but the words wouldn't come out? Have you ever been so frightened that all you could do was cry out, "O God"?

That's happened to me a few times. It happened when my father was dying, and I leaned against the wall and started weeping. I tried to pray, but I couldn't. I was going to seminary to learn to be a pastor, but I couldn't pray that day. No words came out. I didn't know what to say. All I could do was cry out, "O God."

The night when my first son was born, Marlene had been in labor for many hours. The night had started well, but the labor went on and on and on. "Something is wrong on the inside. We've got to get that baby out now," the doctor said. I remember the grim look in his eyes and the fear on Marlene's face. I tried to pray, but I couldn't. I was more frightened at that moment than at any time in my life. All I could say was, "O Lord, have mercy."

That leads me to make this observation: *the more you care about something, the harder it is to pray for it.* The reason we can pray so easily for others is that we're not that deeply invested in them. It's easy to pray for people you don't know because it doesn't matter that much whether or not your prayers are answered. *The more you care, the harder it is to pray.* When it comes to those things in your life that really matter—your husband, your wife, your children, your deepest dreams—those things are hard to pray for because they are so close to your heart.

Paul is saying that in your weakness, when you feel desperate about the things that truly matter to you, and you don't know what to say, and all you can do is cry out "O God!" don't worry. That's enough, because the Holy Spirit is praying for you.

We know that Jesus is in heaven praying for us. But Paul goes a step beyond that. When you come to the moment of complete exhaustion and can no longer frame the words, you don't have to fret. *The Holy Spirit will pray for you.* In your weakness He is strong. When you cannot speak, He speaks for you.

When we lean against the wall of desperation, crying out to God, when we whisper, "God, I don't know what to say. I don't know how to pray about this," the Holy Spirit comes alongside and says, "Don't worry. I'll pray for you."

MARTIN LUTHER'S COMMENT

As I studied this text, I got some help from Martin Luther. Writing some 450 years ago, he said that it is a good thing if you occasionally receive the opposite of what you pray for because that's a sign the Holy Spirit is at work in your life. I find that suggestion to be most encouraging because so many times our prayers—even in our best moments—are tinged with selfish motives. Rarely do we pray from a truly selfless point of view. We may be praying, "Lord, please do this and this and this." Meanwhile, the Holy Spirit inside is saying, "Lord, if he saw the bigger picture, he'd really ask for such-and-such." As we pray from our weak and limited perspective, the Holy Spirit "corrects" our prayers, so to speak, so that God's will is always done, even in our most wrong-headed prayers. Since the Holy Spirit knows what God's will is, and since He "searches our hearts" (see v. 27), He is able to pray for us in ways that always correspond with God's will.

Does that mean our prayers are in vain? Not at all. Does it mean we shouldn't pray? Not at all. *It simply reveals our inherent human weakness and the limitations of our perspective on life.* We see the part; the Holy Spirit sees the whole. We see one little piece; the Holy Spirit sees the big picture. We pray according to the little bit that we see; the Holy Spirit prays according to His perfect knowledge.

Let's wrap up this chapter by drawing three positive conclusions regarding the role of suffering in the Christian life.

CONCLUSION #1:
Suffering is a necessary part of doing God's will

Suffering is part of the Christian experience as we journey from earth to heaven. That means that suffering is a necessary part of doing God's will on earth. For Abraham it meant offering his son Isaac. For Daniel it meant sleeping with the lions. For Paul it meant being stoned and left for dead. For Jesus it meant going to the cross. If you are going through a hard time right now, you don't need anyone to make things worse. Just know that your suffering is part of God's plan for your life, and it therefore places you in some pretty good company.

CONCLUSION #2:
God uses our present suffering to prepare us for future glory

That's the big message of Romans 8. *This life is Basic Training for eternity.* God is using everything that happens in your life—including those things that seem utterly senseless—to prepare you for future glory. In this life we won't know the answer to the question why. But in the life to come we will either know the answer or it won't matter because the glory will be so great that we will simply forget the pain of the past. Either way we will end up completely satisfied.

CONCLUSION #3:
In the meantime we know that our suffering can never separate us from the love of God in Christ Jesus

If in all that I have said you can't find any comfort, hang on to this: God still loves you. He loves you as much in the darkness as He does in the light. Nothing you are going through or ever can go through can separate you from the love of God in Christ Jesus (see Romans 8:35-39). Remember, too, the words of Psalm 34:18, "The Lord is close to the brokenhearted and saves those who are crushed in spirit."

With that thought, let us keep going for the Lord. Be encouraged, child of God. He loves you even in the midst of your pain. He loves you even when you don't love Him. He loves you when you feel utterly alone. He loves you with an everlasting love. Your suffering can take many things away from you—your health, your happiness, your prosperity, your popularity, your friends, your career, even your family. But there's one thing suffering can't take away: it can't take away the love of God.

QUESTIONS FOR PERSONAL/GROUP STUDY

1. Let's consider the four common responses to suffering: denial; anger; blaming others; accepting it and growing from it. Do you know people who respond to suffering the first three ways? Have you ever used those responses yourself? Why is acceptance so difficult? Why is it also necessary?

2. What difference does it make to someone dying of cancer to know that "our suffering is temporary"? Is it a cop-out to say such a thing since suffering for some people won't end until they get to heaven?

3. Why is hope such an important part of the Christian response to suffering? Write down at least three reasons why a Christian can have hope even in the midst of great personal difficulty.

4. Have you found yourself unable to pray during a moment of crisis? Describe that time. What does it mean to you personally to know that the Holy Spirit prays for you in moments like that?

5. Do you find it hard to pray for the things you care most about? Why or why not?

6. Take a look at your prayer list, and pick out the toughest circumstance you face. Spend some time thanking God that His Holy Spirit is at work in that situation in ways you can't even imagine. Ask God to give you grace to patiently wait for His answer.

GOING DEEPER

One popular view today says that suffering is never God's will for the Christian. Some go so far as to suggest that "accepting" suffering is a sub-Christian view that dishonors God, who wants His children to always enjoy health, wealth, and prosperity. How would you respond to that view? Make a list of the people you've known whose faith has grown stronger through the suffering they have endured.

QUESTIONS FOR PERSONAL/GROUP STUDY

1. Let's consider the four common responses to suffering: denial, anger, blaming others, accepting it, and growing from it. Do you know people who respond to suffering the first three ways? Have you ever used those responses yourself? Why is acceptance so difficult? Why is it also necessary?

2. What difference does it make to someone dying of cancer to know that "our suffering is temporary"? Is it a cop-out to say such a thing since suffering for some people won't end until they get to heaven?

3. Why is hope such an important part of the Christian response to suffering? Write down at least three reasons why a Christian can have hope even in the midst of great personal difficulty.

4. Have you found yourself unable to pray during a moment of crisis? What does it mean to you personally to know that the Holy Spirit prays for you in moments like that?

5. Do you find it hard to pray for the things you care most about? Why or why not?

6. Take a look at your prayer list and pick out the toughest circumstance you face. Spend some time thanking God that His Holy Spirit is at work in that situation in ways you can't even imagine. Ask God to give you grace to patiently wait for His answer.

GOING DEEPER

One popular view today says that suffering is never God's will for the Christian. Some go so far as to suggest that "accepting" suffering is a sub-Christian view that dishonors God, who wants His children to always enjoy health, wealth, and prosperity. How would you respond to that view? Make a list of the people you've known whose faith has grown stronger through the suffering they have endured.

CHAPTER NINE

When Christians Disagree

I live in a suburb of Chicago called Oak Park. Approximately 55,000 people live here. On almost every street corner you will find a massive church structure. At the turn of the century, when Oak Park was the first affluent suburb on the railroad west from Chicago, the men driving the delivery wagons said it was easy to know when you entered Oak Park: "It's where the saloons end and the steeples begin."

When the drivers coined that phrase, they were saying Oak Park was a community filled with churches. A century later that observation is still true. Today there are fifty-five different churches there representing over twenty denominations.

But what is true of Oak Park is true of many communities. Across America there are four hundred major denominations. There are over thirty different kinds of Baptists, more than a dozen varieties of Methodists, not to mention a large number of Presbyterian and Lutheran churches. Although we often sing, "We are not divided / All one body we," the many divisions within Christendom show that we don't always mean it.

NOT A NEW PROBLEM

In light of that reality, the question in this chapter is quite narrowly focused: *how do you discover God's will in areas where Christians disagree?*

143

As we begin our discussion, let's start with the observation that Christians have been disagreeing with each other since the very beginning. In fact, the New Testament itself records some of the early arguments among believers. When you read Romans and 1 Corinthians you discover that Christians disagreed on things like eating meat offered to idols, on whether or not to observe the Sabbath Day, on whether to eat meat or be a vegetarian, and on whether or not to drink wine. In Colosse the church was torn by controversy over the proper role of angels, New Moon celebrations, and the proper diet for spiritual Christians. In Thessalonica the young church was deeply confused about the second coming of Christ. In Philippi there was evidently a major power struggle within the church, which is why Philippians contains such a strong plea for unity.

FUNDAMENTAL THINGS

I should stop at this point and say plainly that there are some doctrines that Christians have always believed. These are fundamental issues having to do with the Trinity, the deity of Jesus Christ and His virgin birth, sinless life, atoning death, and bodily resurrection, the nature of the Bible as God's inerrant Word, salvation by grace through faith, the certainty of the second coming of Christ, the resurrection of the dead, and the reality of eternal life through Jesus Christ. While the precise wording has often differed, and while some groups have emphasized one doctrine over another, true Christians have always affirmed these central doctrines.

In this chapter I am not speaking about disagreements over these fundamental, non-negotiable doctrines. These truths are not "up for grabs," as if we could take or leave whether or not to believe that Jesus is God or the Second Coming. Those truths belong to the "faith that was once for all entrusted to the saints" (Jude 3).

In this chapter we are looking at what we might call Category 2 disagreements—areas of doctrine or practice not involving the fundamentals of the Christian faith.

REFLECTIONS ON AN ANCIENT QUARREL

That brings us back to the basic question: how do you determine God's will in those areas where Christians disagree? In order to help us answer that question, let's study the record of an ancient quarrel between two old friends. Acts 15:36-41 tells the story of the disagreement between Paul and Barnabas. We pick up the story in verse 36:

> Some time later Paul said to Barnabas, "Let us go back and visit the brothers in all the towns where we preached the word of the Lord and see how they are doing." Barnabas wanted to take John, also called Mark, with them, but Paul did not think it wise to take him, because he had deserted them in Pamphylia and had not continued with them in the work.

Don't rush past that last sentence. It's a reference to an incident that took place on their first missionary journey. Three of them had gone out together—Paul, Barnabas, and Barnabas' young cousin, John Mark. In their travels they came to Pamphylia, a coastal province of Asia Minor. Luke tells the story this way in Acts 13:13-14: "From Paphos, Paul and his companions sailed to Perga in Pamphylia, where John left them to return to Jerusalem. From Perga they went on to Pisidian Antioch." The most interesting fact about this passage is what it doesn't say. We can't be sure why John Mark left the team and returned to Jerusalem. In looking at the itinerary, it's clear that the easiest part of the journey was behind them. Ahead lay long mountain treks into possibly unfriendly towns. Perhaps it was more than John Mark bargained for. Perhaps he couldn't get along with Paul. Who knows? Maybe he felt that his cousin Barnabas should be the leader. Perhaps he was homesick for Jerusalem. Luke's spartan prose records the facts but nothing more. From reading these words you would not infer any problems behind the scenes.

But this much is true: at a crucial moment John Mark suddenly left the team. No one knows the exact reason, but one day he said, "I'm leaving." So he left Paul and Barnabas behind and returned home.

When the time came for the second trip Barnabas said, "Let's give him a another chance." To which Paul replied, "Forget it.

We're not taking him." So they argued over whether to take John Mark with them on the second trip. We pick up the story in Acts 15:39.

> They had such a sharp disagreement that they parted company. Barnabas took Mark and sailed for Cyprus, but Paul chose Silas and left, commended by the brothers to the grace of the Lord. He went through Syria and Cilicia, strengthening the churches.

In the end Paul and Barnabas disagreed so sharply that they finally decided to go their separate ways. Paul found a replacement for Barnabas (a man named Silas) and went north toward Asia Minor. Barnabas took John Mark and sailed west toward Cyprus. Having found no way to patch up their quarrel, they separated and went their own ways.

Using this passage as a base, I want to share with you seven principles that will help you discern God's will in areas where Christians disagree.

PRINCIPLE #1:
Though all Christians worship the same Lord, we don't always agree on every point

If you've been around the evangelical church very long, you know that we disagree on almost everything. Recently I made a list of *some* of the things Christians disagree about:

Hollywood movies
Drinking wine
Watching TV
Eating out on Sunday
Billy Graham crusades
Playing cards
Women wearing head coverings in church
The *King James Version*
Picketing abortion clinics
Men wearing beards
Using credit cards
Divorced men serving as ushers
Home schooling
Mixed swimming

Women wearing pants to church
Smoking
Rock music
Christian rock music
Christian rock music in church
Long hair on men
Short hair on women
Women working outside the home
Birth control
Guitars in a church service
Working in a restaurant where liquor is served

Christian schools vs. public schools
Speaking in tongues
R-rated movies
Christian-sponsored boycotts
Sex education
Rush Limbaugh
The ecumenical movement
Playing the saxophone in church
Halloween
Interracial marriage
Christians in politics
Sunday night services
True Christians in liberal churches
Seeker services
The Lord's supper
Christian counseling
Twelve-step programs
Mode of baptism
Faith-promise giving
Women wearing makeup
Clapping in church
Traditional vs. contemporary worship

I will offer two observations about that long list. Number 1: in the greater body of Christ *you will find genuine, heartfelt disagreement over every one of these issues*. The fact that you found part of that list funny just means that some of those things don't bother you, but for each item you could find someone (usually some group of people) who feel strongly about it.

The second observation is this: *there is disagreement about some of those issues in every church*. For instance, as you read the different items, you probably said to yourself, "Well, that's silly . . . I can't believe anyone worries about that." If we took ten people and asked each one to make a list of the things that are silly and the things that are genuine issues, none of the lists would be identical.

PRINCIPLE #2:
On issues of deep personal conviction, our disagreements will sometimes be very sharp

Let's go back to Acts 15. Verse 39 tells us that Paul and Barnabas had "a sharp disagreement." The Greek text uses a word from which we get the English word *paroxysm*, which means a violent disagreement. This particular Greek word means a violent, hostile, angry, harsh, sharp, bitter disagreement. It's not as if Barnabas said, "Well, I would like to take Mark." "I'm not sure that's a good idea." "But he's such a fine boy." "But he left us." "Let's pray about it." No! They weren't that nice about it. In fact, the verb is in the imperfect tense, which means a continual quarrel—an unending, unyielding, ongoing, heated, intense, deep disagreement between them.

Their argument was continual and it was contentious. They didn't just argue once and then let it go. They argued over and over again. And the more they argued, the angrier they got. Barnabas *knew* he was right. And Paul *knew* he was right.

That raises a critical question: Was Barnabas right or was Paul?

PAUL LOOKED AT THE MINISTRY

After studying the matter, I have concluded you can make a good case either way. *I believe Paul was thinking about the ministry.* He had the big picture in mind. He was thinking about the fact that they were about to leave on a missionary trip. This was no Sunday school picnic. They were going into uncharted territory to take the Gospel to lost people. They were going into mountainous regions. They were going to places where they would face death every day. On the first missionary journey—the one John Mark had left— Paul was stoned and left for dead in Lystra. They could hardly expect anything better this time around. They would encounter opposition, persecution, hardship, and sickness. Paul knew there was no place for a quitter on a trip like that. Paul focused on the people he was trying to reach. He couldn't take the risk of having John Mark walk out on him again. He needed someone he could depend on 100 percent. That's what I mean when I say that Paul was looking at the ministry.

BARNABAS LOOKED AT THE MAN

We know that John Mark was his cousin, which means there were family issues to consider. When Barnabas looked at his young cousin, he said, "We serve a God of grace. He is the God of the second chance. Our God never gives up on anybody." Barnabas saw real potential in his young cousin, though he had turned away when things got rough. "Paul, maybe you've written this guy off. But I'm not writing him off because God hasn't written him off. I believe in him even though he has failed. I want to give him another chance."

So who do you think was right? *Your answer tells us a whole lot more about you than about this text of Scripture.* I don't think the Bible clearly tells us who was right or wrong here. But everybody has an opinion. If you're people-oriented, you'll probably move toward Barnabas. If you're task-oriented, you may side with Paul.

Regardless of who was right or wrong, we know that there was a sharp, almost violent disagreement between these two men. That leads us directly to the third principle.

PRINCIPLE #3:
Separation may ultimately be preferable to continual disagreement

When Paul and Barnabas couldn't agree, only one solution remained: they split up and went in separate directions. Verse 39 says, "they parted company." That's a weak translation. The word in Greek means "to part asunder." *It means a total break in the relationship.* They were so angry that when they left, they didn't just part company—their friendship at that point was torn apart.

As far as we can tell from this text, when Barnabas went one way and Paul the other, they evidently left unreconciled. Nothing in the text indicates that they got on their knees and prayed together. Maybe they did, but I don't see it. All I see is a sharp dis-agreement and a separation. There's no happy ending here.

At this point it's important for us to review the biblical teach-ing on unity. I find it interesting that Paul—the man who didn't want to take John Mark—writes more about the unity of the church than any other man in the New Testament. Do you remember what he says?

> Be devoted to one another in brotherly love (Romans 12:10).

> Live in harmony with one another (Romans 12:16).

> If it is possible, as far as it depends on you, live at peace with every-one (Romans 12:18).

> Make every effort to keep the unity of the Spirit through the bond of peace (Ephesians 4:3).

> Make my joy complete by being like-minded, having the same love,
> being one in spirit and purpose (Philippians 2:2).

> Bear with each other and forgive whatever grievances you may have
> against one another. Forgive as the Lord forgave you (Colossians
> 3:13).

All those verses came from the pen of the Apostle Paul. I find
that phrase in Romans 12:18 very interesting: "if it is possible."
Sometimes outward unity isn't possible. This is hard for some of us to
admit. Sometimes separation may ultimately be preferable to continual, unending quarreling and disagreement. If Paul and Barnabas
couldn't agree, then perhaps we won't always agree either.

We can summarize the matter this way: the command to maintain unity is always there. But sometimes we will have to obey it
separately.

In that light this text is helpful because it is so brutally honest
about two men and their disagreement. Isn't it interesting that
Luke includes this in the Book of Acts? He could have glossed
over the whole ugly affair; but he chose to tell the truth. This text
is very honest. It's also very comforting because it tells us that the
men of the Bible were not angels. They were men with strong
feelings and with strong convictions.

PRINCIPLE #4:
God's Word is sometimes advanced
through disagreement

Let's do a simple before and after analysis:

Before	After
Two men	Five men
One team	Two teams
One place	Two places

Before the trouble, there were two men (Paul, Barnabas) on
one team headed for one place (Asia Minor). After the argument
was over, there were five men (Paul, Silas, Timothy, Barnabas,
John Mark) on two teams going to two different places (Cyprus,

Asia Minor). Thus the Gospel was now being spread by more people in more places than before. *That happened as a result of a sharp, strong, personal disagreement.*

Let's add Romans 8:28 to the equation—"And we know that in all things"—even our sharp disagreements—"God works for the good of those who love him." This does not justify anger or bitterness, but it does illustrate the biblical principle that God is able to make the wrath of man praise him.

Throughout church history, the Christian movement has often grown through disagreement. For instance, the Reformation started over a disagreement about justification by faith. The record is clear that Martin Luther never intended to start a new church. He truly meant to reform the existing church. But when the Roman Catholic Church booted him out, he established churches based on the teaching of justification by faith, and from that beginning the Gospel spread to the ends of the earth.

I'm not in favor of church splits. But God is able to use disagreements to advance the cause of Christ. Eighty years ago the church I pastor was started by some people who were members of mainline churches in Oak Park. They didn't march in the streets or picket the liberal churches; they just determined to start a new congregation. The result was Calvary Memorial Church. That church exists because someone disagreed with what was going on in other churches. Separation—as painful as it may be— sometimes can be used for the advancement of the Gospel.

GOD USES THE WORST

Let me make a personal application at this point. *The Holy Spirit often uses conflict, disagreement, and disappointment to reveal God's will to the individual believer.* God is able to work through even the most painful experiences of life not only to bless you, but to prepare you and to enable you to move on to the place where he wants you to be.

I have seen that principle at work in my own life. Years ago I came to a moment of serious disagreement with two Christian brothers. Months of pressure culminated in a late-night meeting that almost ended in blows. Awful things were said, unkind words spoken, harsh judgments made, friendships broken. When it was over, I went through a painful period during which I faced my own sin and failure. Months later God used that terrible moment to pry me loose from one place and set my feet going in a new direction.

God is able to use the worst parts of life to show us His will. Nothing is wasted with our Heavenly Father. Out of the ashes of defeat we hear the voice of God. When the battle is over, when tempers have cooled, when our anger is gone, we hear the voice of the Lord saying, "Now follow Me, and I will be your guide."

PRINCIPLE #5:
If we must separate from one another, let us do so with respect, not with rancor

Rancor means anger or bitterness. I think if there is any place to criticize Paul and Barnabas, it's right here. *It seems to me that perhaps they went too far in their disagreement.*

It's not a sin to disagree. We don't have to agree on everything. You want to play a saxophone on Sunday morning? That's okay. Want to go fishing? Go fishing. Want to wear pants, grow a beard, home school your kids, listen to Rush Limbaugh, join the Democratic Party, buy a pipe organ, show Billy Graham films in the sanctuary, or argue against women ushers? Go right ahead. We don't have to agree on every detail.

But we can disagree without being disagreeable. If there is one mistake that Paul and Barnabas made, it's that they may have crossed the line from strong disagreement into something that became too personal.

THREE WARNING SIGNS

The danger is that not only will we disagree and separate, but that we'll cross the line from justifiable disagreement to anger and bitterness. Let me share three warning signs to help you know when you've crossed that line.

#1: *When the issue becomes a controlling passion of your life.* You've crossed the line when all you do is lie awake at night thinking about that saxophone on Sunday morning. You wake up in the middle of the night, and you can just hear that saxophone blaring "A Mighty Fortress Is Our God," and it bothers you. That's all you can think about; it's all you can talk about during the day. You've gone too far when the issue—whatever it is—becomes the controlling passion in your life.

#2: When you begin to attack the person and not the problem. Attacking the problem means studying the issue, sorting out the good and bad points, thinking through other ways of looking at things, and so on. Attacking the person means losing your temper, questioning motives, and using intimidation to get your own way. When it gets personal, you've gone too far. In the heat of controversy it's easy to spread rumors or tell stories or twist facts in order to make someone else look bad. At that point you've gone way over the line. It doesn't matter how big or how little the issue is, you ought to be able to discuss it rationally without stooping to rumor and character assassination.

#3: When you would rather talk about "your issue" than about Jesus Christ. This is often where Christian disagreement ends up. Somehow Jesus becomes a casualty of our in-fighting. Sometimes our message to the world seems to be, "God loves you, but we hate each other." Too often we fight so much about secondary things that Jesus gets pushed over to the side. Is it any wonder that the world shrugs off our message? When you would rather fight other Christians than share Christ with the lost, something has gone wrong in your spiritual life.

So if we have to disagree—and sometimes we do, and if we have to go our separate ways—and sometimes we do, then may we disagree agreeably—with respect and not rancor.

PRINCIPLE #6:
In Christ our ultimate goal should be eventual reconciliation and the restoration of friendship

This doesn't come easily. I know exactly what I'm talking about at this point. From personal experience I can tell you that it's not easy to restore fellowship with brothers who have been offended. As one who has been on both sides of that fence—the offender and the offended—I can testify to how difficult reconciliation is. But I think that's what the Christian Gospel is all about.

Let's go back to the story in Acts 15–16. The argument is over; nothing more needs to be said. Both men are angry, hurt, and frustrated. There is nothing left to do but to go their separate ways. Paul goes north; Barnabas goes west. They separate, and as far as we know they don't meet again for years.

Time passes, tempers cool down, a new perspective comes, they begin to see things in a different light, and the Holy Spirit does His healing work.

Let's run the clock ahead about ten years. How does Paul feel about Barnabas now? We have only one hint. In 1 Corinthians 9:1-6 he mentions Barnabas as a fellow apostle and a fellow worker in the cause of Jesus Christ. Ten years pass from the time of the argument, and Paul is able to look at Barnabas and say, "My friend, my fellow apostle, my partner, my coworker." Something had happened to bring about reconciliation and healing.

A QUITTER BECOMES A TRUSTED FRIEND

Paul thought John Mark was a quitter. Did he ever change his opinion? Two passages of Scripture answer that question. Fifteen years have passed, and Paul is imprisoned in Rome. At the end of his letter to the Colossians, he adds these telling words: "My fellow prisoner Aristarchus sends you his greetings, as does Mark, the cousin of Barnabas" (4:10). John Mark and Paul are not only friends, but now that Paul is in prison, who's there taking care of him? That quitter, John Mark.

Three more years pass. Paul is in jail for the last time. Soon he will be put to death. From his prison cell in Rome he writes to his young friend Timothy. These are his last recorded words in Scripture. In 2 Timothy 4, Paul talks about the fact that so many people have left him—"Demas . . . has deserted me. . . . Crescens has gone to Galatia, and Titus to Dalmatia. Only Luke is with me. Get Mark and bring him with you, because he is helpful to me in my ministry" (4:11). In his last days Paul wanted John Mark by his side. What a change from his earlier opinion. Once Paul didn't want anything to do with him because he thought he was a loser. But at the end of his life, Paul says, "Bring him to me. I need him."

That's what the Gospel of Jesus Christ can do. *Sometimes our disagreements seem so deep that we think we are separated forever.* But because we're still in the family of God, there's always the possibility of reconciliation.

THE MARK OF THE CHRISTIAN

God used Francis Schaeffer to communicate the gospel to millions of people. Included among his works is a little book called *The Mark of the Christian.* In it he argued that love must be the defining mark of the Christian. That's the label we must wear in all our relationships. From that book I learned an important truth: *the world is not looking for outward unity but outward love.* We'll disagree on a thousand secondary issues. That's okay as long as we love each other. If we disagree, we can disagree agreeably and thus demonstrate that we are still part of God's great family. If we must disagree, even if we must separate, we must disagree with respect and not with rancor.

I would also add that in dealing with secondary issues, we must always hold out the possibility of future reconciliation. How do you do that? *The most important factor involved in reconciliation is time. Give God time to soften hearts.* That may mean waiting months or years before the disagreeing parties can be brought back together. Time doesn't heal all wounds, but sometimes the passage of time allows a new perspective to develop. Eventually those issues that once seemed so important begin to recede into the background. Perhaps you will conclude that, yes, they were important at a given time and place, but they aren't so important now.

Beyond that, it's important not to continually bring up past disagreements. *As long as you live in the past, you're going to be fighting in the past.* Eventually you have to move out of the past and into the present. That involves a conscious choice to forgive those who, in a time of conflict, brutalized you. It's not easy to do that; but with the help of the Holy Spirit, you can rise above past hurts to discover the joy of reconciliation.

That brings us to one final principle.

PRINCIPLE #7:
Hold your convictions firmly yet graciously, knowing that God may lead someone else differently than He has led you

What an important truth for the family of God. Romans 14:5 says that "each one should be fully convinced in his own mind." If you want a beard, grow one. Do you like your pastors clean-shaven? Fine! Hold on to that. If you're a home schooler, be fully convinced. Do you prefer the public schools? That's wonderful. What about Christian schools? Great! Nothing I am saying implies that you shouldn't have convictions. You should.

But that's only part of it. Romans 15:5-6 offers the other side of the coin: "May the God who gives endurance and encouragement give you a spirit of unity among yourselves as you follow Christ Jesus, so that with one heart and mouth you may glorify the God and Father of our Lord Jesus Christ." *God places a high value on Christian unity*. Hold on to your convictions, but do it in a loving fashion. After all, your convictions may change over time. What you oppose so strongly today may, in a different context, become less than crucial to you in the future.

We're different, and that's okay. We don't agree on everything, and that's okay. Sometimes in the family of God we're going to disagree strongly, and that's okay. Sometimes we're going to disagree to the point that we can't even work together anymore. That's okay too. Sometimes we're going to go our separate ways, and that's okay. We don't all have to go to the same church or belong to the same denomination or believe the same way on controversial *secondary* issues.

But we do have to love one another. That's a non-negotiable command of Jesus Christ (John 13:34). *No matter how much or how passionately we disagree, we still must love each other.*

PARTLY RIGHT, PARTLY WRONG

Here's a simple, five-step outline for discovering God's will in doubtful areas where Christians disagree:

Step #1: Pray for guidance.
Step #2: Search the Scriptures.
Step #3: Seek godly counsel.
Step #4: Ask God to give you specific direction.
Step #5: Decide what you believe.

And don't grumble when others see things differently. Do what you believe to be right before the Lord, and let God worry about those other people.

That brings me back to the question I asked earlier in this chapter: who was right—Paul or Barnabas? I don't think the Bible really answers that question. But I'm glad about that. So many of our arguments end up the same way. When it's all over, you're not totally sure who's right. Even after you study both sides, you can see some points here and points there. As long we live in a fallen world, most of our disagreements will end up that way.

Dr. Robert Lightner tells of a practice used by Japanese parents when their children fight with one another. They bring each child into the room and put a square cushion on the table. One by one each child puts his hands on the cushion and says, "I am right, and my friend is wrong." He then moves to the other side, puts his hands on it, and says, "My friend is right, and I am wrong." The child then places his hands on the third side of the cushion, saying, "Both of us are right, and both of us are wrong." As he places his hands on the final side, he very thoughtfully says, "I am partly right, and my friend is partly right."

When we get to heaven and look back on many of the issues that have divided us, we will say the same thing. *We were partly right, and our friends were partly right.* Between now and then there are going to be plenty of disagreements in the church. That goes with being human. But we have the opportunity to deal with our disagreements honestly and graciously because we know Jesus Christ. He makes the difference.

What do you do when Christians disagree? Hold your convictions, but hold them in love.

QUESTIONS FOR PERSONAL/GROUP STUDY

1. Take a look at the list of "debatable issues." Put a plus by the ones that seem to be legitimate issues to you and a minus by the ones that seem trivial to you. Was there a time when your tally would have been different? Why? What does that tell you about yourself? About the whole area of Category 2 disagreements?

2. So who was right—Paul or Barnabas? Pick a side and defend it. If you feel strongly one way or the other, can you see *any* legitimate reasons why someone else would favor the other man?

3. How can the statement that "separation is sometimes preferable" be reconciled with the scriptural command to "keep the unity of the Spirit through the bond of peace"?

4. What issues are important enough to make you break a friendship with another Christian, leave your church, or change denominations?

5. Why is it so hard for Christians to "disagree agreeably"? Is that even possible, given the strong feelings we have on many issues?

6. Why does the New Testament put such a high value on loving other Christians and keeping unity in the body of Christ? Given the many differences of opinion within the Christian church, how can we maintain the integrity of our convictions and yet demonstrate love for one another? Be specific.

GOING DEEPER

Perhaps it's time to take a personal inventory of your own life. Are you better at "keeping the unity" or "standing for the truth"? Can you think of any times in your life when you have "crossed the line" and become too focused on a particular issue? Have you ever separated from a Christian friend over an issue, only to regret it later? Have you ever regretted not taking a stand over an issue of importance? Would you call yourself more of a "Paul" or more of a "Barnabas"? Why?

CHAPTER TEN

Trapped on a Dead-end Street

This morning a friend called with some bad news. A few months ago a pastor had resigned from his church saying that he was burned out. Later he moved with his wife to another state. Only then did the truth come out. He had been having an affair with a younger woman. When she demanded that he divorce his wife and marry her, he decided to leave the area. But she revealed the story of the affair, which led to a sad series of events culminating in the pastor leaving his wife of many years to live with the other woman. As I write these words, the pastor and his lover are planning to divorce their mates and marry each other.

The story doesn't end there, however. Evidently this isn't the first time, or the first woman, or the first case of adultery, or the first church he has deceived. This man has engaged in a pattern of sinful behavior over a period of years, which has now resulted in two broken marriages, a wonderful church humiliated, hundreds of innocent people hurt, and the name of Christ stained by the deliberate sin of a Christian leader.

I do not write these words out of anger. Every time I hear such a story I recall the solemn words of 1 Corinthians 10:12, "So, if you think you are standing firm, be careful that you don't fall." Could it have been me? In my heart I know the answer is yes. I have felt the same temptation many times. Every pastor has.

But that's not the issue. The sin does not consist of feeling the pressure but yielding to temptation.

This chapter is not about pastoral indiscretions, though I could add story after story to the one I just told. Nor is it about sexual infidelity, though the Bible has a great deal to say about that subject. No; this chapter is about finding God's will when you are out of God's will. It's about what to do when you have done wrong.

FAR AWAY FROM GOD

Let's begin with a very simple observation: *it is possible to know God and yet be far away from Him.* Most Christians know the truth of that statement from personal experience. The journey from earth to heaven rarely runs straight. For most people, the path is filled with twists and turns and unexplainable switchbacks. As all rock climbers know, you never reach the summit without going up, then down, then sideways, searching for that elusive path that leads you to the top. Sometimes you find yourself trapped halfway up what seemed like a promising short-cut. At that moment you either decide to stay where you are (not a very attractive possibility) or you slowly, carefully begin to find your way out of danger.

Something like that happens to many believers in their journey with Jesus Christ. Out of frustration or desperation or anger or sometimes sheer bullheadedness, they look for a short-cut that will get them where they want to go.

Perhaps you have had the experience of drifting away from God. You never meant it to happen. You didn't start intending to drift away from the Lord. But somewhere along the way you made some wrong choices, and one day you woke up to find that you were far away from God.

This is something that happens irrespective of your spiritual pedigree. You might be a pastor or an elder or a deacon and still be a long way from God. You might be a Sunday school teacher, a youth leader, an usher, a member of the choir, a student at a Christian college, and still be far away from God. You may have been raised in a Christian home, only to grow up and reject your heritage. You may have been deeply hurt by someone who claimed to be a

Christian, and that grievous wound has kept you from coming close to God. You may have decided that no one can truly live up to what the Bible commands. Perhaps you feel discouraged over repeated personal failure. You tried and tried and tried . . . and finally, exhausted, you gave up.

A CRUCIAL DISTINCTION

Let's talk about what to do when you realize that you are out of God's will. Before going on, we need to carefully distinguish between two different ways we use that phrase, "out of God's will." *Sometimes we use it to describe decisions we would like to make over again.* You bought a new house, but now you don't like it. You went to work right out of high school, but you wish now that you had gone to college. You blew $3,000 on a hot tip because your friend said the stock was bound to go up, but the stock dropped 31 points. Twenty years ago you had a chance to marry the nicest man you ever knew, but for some reason you said no, and one day he married someone else. Now you wish you had acted decisively when you had the chance.

Those examples describe *non-moral decisions*, decisions about which the Bible gives no direct guidance. *You are free to make those decisions any way you like.* You can stay in school or quit, buy the stock or not, buy a mini-van or keep the car you already have. You are free to invest the money or not, as you see fit. You are free to get married or to remain single. The Bible doesn't tell you what to do in situations like that.

There is, however, a second common use of the phrase, "out of God's will." *It refers to those times when you suffer because you have done that which is wrong in the eyes of the Lord.* It refers to those times when you suffer personally, internally, relationally, emotionally, and in every other area of your life because you have sinned against God.

You committed adultery, and now you are out of God's will. You had an abortion, and now you are out of God's will. You assassinated somebody's character, and now you are out of God's will. You are nursing a grudge and a bitter spirit, and you are out of God's will. You killed somebody. You lied. You stole. You cheated.

You extorted money. You deliberately hurt other people. As a result you are out of God's will.

You wonder, "What do I do now?" *Somewhere along the way you walked through the wrong door.* The only way back to God's will is to go back through that same door. You decided to leave God's will; you must now decide to return to God's will. You left on purpose; you must return on purpose.

THE GREATEST SHORT STORY EVER TOLD

Jesus told a story about a young man who made a wrong decision and what happened to him as a result. We call it the Parable of the Prodigal Son. Many people consider it the greatest short story ever written because it speaks so truthfully to the human condition.

The parable is the story of a father with two sons. The younger son chafes under his father's rule and perhaps feels put down by his obedient older brother. So he demands his inheritance from his father, who agrees to give it to him. Taking the money, he leaves home and journeys to a place the Bible calls "a far country" (KJV). There he spends every dime he has on riotous living. Parties day and night, women on both arms, the good life, the fast lane. Whatever he wants, he buys with his father's money. Eventually the money runs out. When a famine comes, not having any money and being too far away from home, he attaches himself to a farmer who says, "The only work I have is feeding my pigs." The prodigal son ends up penniless, homeless, starving, feeding swine, eating the pods from the carob trees. He who had eaten prime rib just a few weeks earlier now dines with the pigs.

Before going any farther with the story, let's stop and analyze what happened to this young man. How did he end up in such a mess?

FIVE STEPS TO THE PIGPEN

1. *He was selfish.* His fall began with a selfish act, a disregard for his father. He said, "I want my money, and I want it now." All he could see were the dollar signs. "Dad, give me my money. Forget you, and forget my family. Forget my brother. Forget my reputation. Give me my money. I want to get out of here."

2. *He acted hastily.* The Bible says that when he got his money he went to "a far country." When you hear that phrase, you shouldn't think of somewhere thousands of miles away. Do you know where the far country is? It's *one step outside God's will.* You could be living in your own home and still be in "a far country." It's not a matter of geography, but of a broken relationship with God.

3. *He wasted everything he had.* The word *prodigal* means "wasteful." When he left, he never intended to come back home. After all, he took all the money with him. If he had planned to return, he would have left some money behind. But, no—he deliberately did what he did. He wasn't tricked into spending his money. He left home intending to spend it all.

4. *He separated himself from every relationship that was important to him.* By leaving, he broke his relationship with his father and his brother. He left his family and his friends. He rejected everything that was good and right and holy. All of that went out the window.

5. *He made a long string of bad decisions.* Sin always works that way. One bad decision leads to another. First you tell a lie, then you have to tell another one to cover up the first one, then another one to cover up the second one, and then another one to cover up the third one. *Sin always leads to more sin.* Once you start making bad decisions, it's easier to make them as you go along. But pretty soon you are about fifteen bad decisions down the road. At that point it seems easier to keep on going in the wrong direction

Please note what happened next. There was a famine. *Whenever you leave God, there will always be a famine in the far country.* It looks so good, like a land flowing with milk and honey. In the far country you enjoy the pleasures of sin for a season. But after a while the money runs out, the music stops, the beautiful people get bored with you, and you are broke and penniless.

In the end he lost everything. He who had it all lost it all. He who came from a good family now slept with the pigs. The prodigal son had hit rock bottom. *God often lets that happen, because many of us won't look up until we start to eat with the pigs.* When we finally hit rock bottom, then and only then do we begin to think about going home again.

THE WAY BACK HOME

When the prodigal son hit bottom, his life began to change. Five words tell the story.

First, there was an *awakening*. Luke 15:17 says, "When he came to his senses." That's a great phrase—"he came to his senses." Sin is senseless. *Sin is a form of temporary spiritual insanity.* Turning away from living water so you can drink out of a sewer—that is the definition of spiritual insanity.

What was it that brought him to his senses? He was hungry. *His stomach made him come back to his father.* That's not a very exalted motive. Nothing suggests he turned back to his father because he realized what a terrible thing he had done. Ponder that for a moment. As Jesus tells the story, the turning point comes when the young man gets hungry. He hasn't repented yet or come to grips with the enormity of his sin. That's still in the future. I think it's fair to say that if someone in the far country had offered him a meal, he would have taken it and stayed right where he was. Why make the humiliating journey back home if you can get your needs met by living in sin?

Here is a startling truth: *sinners often turn to the Lord simply because they have nowhere else to go.* Their motives may be no more exalted than the need to find a hot meal and a place to stay on a cold night in December. That truth leads to this insight: *when you are praying for a straying believer, ask God to make them hungry.* Pray for the famine to come. Pray for their money to run out. "Lord, make him so miserable that sin no longer looks inviting." "Lord, make her hungry for the love she used to know." "Lord, make him so restless that he can't sleep at night."

Second, there was *repentance*. He said to himself, "I will set out and go back to my father" (v. 18). Repentance is what happens when you've been going the wrong direction and finally you say, "I've gone this way long enough. I'm going to turn around, and I'm going to go back in the other direction." *Repentance is a change of mind that leads to a change of life.*

If the first step back toward home stemmed from personal need, the second one begins to grapple with the root problem. Now the young man realizes that his fundamental need is not for food, but for a restored relationship with his father. He's hungry tonight because many months ago he got greedy and left home. He's sleeping with the pigs because in his pig-headedness he demanded his own way. He's living alone because he chose to leave those who loved him. Repentance means admitting you are solely responsible for the mess you are in. You can't go back home until you admit you were the one who left in the first place.

Third, there was *honesty*. The young man said, "I will set out and go back to my father and say to him: Father, I have sinned against heaven and against you" (v. 18).

You will know you are really serious about changing your life when you stop making excuses for your behavior. Think about what the prodigal son could have said. "It was really my older brother's fault. He always picked on me, and Daddy always liked him best." Or, "If Daddy had given me more money I wouldn't be in this fix." Or, "Those cheap women seduced me and then stole my money. And that farmer never gave me a good job." He could have found a thousand excuses. But he didn't. He simply said, "I have sinned." Those three little words—so simple, so short, yet so profound—marked the beginning of a new life for this young man. When you stop making excuses for your failures, you are not far from a brand-new life.

Fourth, there was *humility*. While he was still in the pigpen, he mentally rehearsed what he would say to his father: "I am no longer worthy to be called your son; make me like one of your hired men" (v. 19). What a tremendous statement that was. *He came back home with no pre-conditions.* He didn't say, "Dad, before I'll come back, we've got to make a deal." He didn't say, "You have to give me exactly what I had. I'm coming back, but I want that fortune I lost. You have to replace it." That's not real repentance. This man was so deeply hurt over the way he had lived that he said, "Father, I'm not worthy to be called your son. I've disgraced you. If you will take me back, I will work like a hired hand." *Real repentance doesn't make deals with God.*

Fifth, there was *resolution*. "So he got up and went to his father" (v. 20). After awakening comes repentance, then honesty, then humility. It all leads to the resolution to go home.

It's certainly easy to criticize the prodigal son. But I will tell you at least one good thing about this young man. *When the time came to move, he moved*. He didn't let the grass grow under his feet. So many people say, "Give me some time to think about it." Not this man. He didn't delay but simply started out on the journey home.

THE FATHER'S WELCOME

As the son shuffled along the road, one question undoubtedly went through his mind: what is my father going to say? Will he take me back? With his head down, he walked along that dirt road, embarrassed and humiliated.

Certainly his fears were well-founded. We don't often think about the father's pain when we read this story. But it couldn't have been easy for him. First of all, he lost part of the fortune he had worked so long to amass. Second, he lost his reputation in the community. When a son leaves home in such anger, there's no way to keep it hidden. The older brother knew, the hired men knew, and soon enough the friends and neighbors knew about it. Every time the father went into town, people talked about it behind his back. Dysfunctional families make good gossip for idle minds. People talked about what had happened, and they analyzed the problems. Perhaps some of the younger men took the son's side. No doubt the older men sided with the father. Meanwhile, the father knew all about the talk, heard the whispers, and through it all silently struggled to keep his dignity.

But the worst pain was the simple fact that the father had lost his son. After all these years, after all those prayers, after holding him in his arms, after teaching him how to hunt and fish, after pouring out an ocean of love, suddenly the dream was shattered, and the father was left with a huge hole in his heart.

Words cannot express the pain, the sadness, the loss the father felt. His son had left home, and no one could console him.

After all that, could anyone blame the father if he refused to take his son back? No wonder the son worried as he slowly plodded toward home. He had no idea what awaited him.

HIS FATHER SAW HIM FIRST

The Bible says that while the son was still a long way off, his father saw him. This is a great moment. *His father saw him first*. His father saw him and was moved with compassion. Day after day the father had watched for his son. Night after night he waited for his return. Nothing deterred him—not the weather, not the jeers and jokes of the skeptics, not the doubting looks of his friends. Deep in his heart he *knew* his son would someday come back home.

Then it happened. One day, late in the afternoon, when the sun was beating down and sweat covered his face, the father saw a figure slowly come over the rise and begin to walk slowly, hesitantly toward him.

Throwing all dignity aside, he ran to meet his son, embraced him without even a word, threw his arms around him, and kissed him. The word Jesus used means he *smothered* him with kisses.

In that one moment all questions were answered. The son's fear melted away in his father's tears and hugs. No words passed between them; one broken heart spoke to another.

Then came the sobbed confession: "Father, I have sinned against heaven and against you. I am no longer worthy to be called your son" (v. 21). Every word was true. The son had sinned against heaven and against his father. Indeed, he had forfeited his legal rights. If the father wanted to make his son a hired hand, no one would lift a hand to stop him. The son had defamed the family name. Who could blame the father if he said, "Don't ever call yourself my son again"?

No one could have predicted what happened next. It is for this that we love this story. We read it over and over again and cling to it, believe it, hope in it, stake our lives upon it—all because of the father's welcome to his erring son.

Notice the five signs of the father's welcome:

1. The kiss—the sign of forgiveness.
2. The robe—the sign of honor.
3. The ring—the sign of authority.
4. The sandals—the sign of freedom.
5. The feast—the sign of a joyful welcome.

Verse 24 brings the first part of the story to a close with these wonderful words of hope: "So they began to celebrate." At the father's command, a party began that lasted for hours. Perhaps you also know about the older brother who refused to join in the celebration. He represents all those right-thinking, right-living rule-keepers who want to see repentant sinners publicly punished to teach them a lesson. Just as the prodigal son still lives today, so does his unhappy older brother.

But how did the father feel about his son who had come home? "We had to celebrate and be glad, because this brother of your was dead and is alive again; he was lost and is found." (v. 32) Back from the dead! Found! Alive again! Home again! No wonder the father said, "Let's have a party."

MODERN-DAY PRODIGALS

How much does God love you?

- He loves you enough to let you go.
- He loves you enough to let you hit bottom.
- He loves you enough to let you come back.
- He loves you so much that He will run to meet you.

That's how much God loves you.

I would like to end this chapter with two stories that I hope will encourage you. Each one tells about a modern-day prodigal son or daughter who after many years finally came home.

About a year ago a letter arrived from a woman who has gone through many personal struggles. The details of her particular "far country" don't matter. What matters is that when she hit bottom, she finally returned to the Lord. With her permission, I am sharing portions of her letter with you.

> I wanted to let you know how grateful to God I am, for His love and discipline and faithfulness to me.
>
> During a time of anger I refused to come to church. When I did come to church everything sounded silly to me or useless. If the message was about hope, I would say in my mind "Why?" or "In what?"
>
> But let me tell you, those chains of fear and anger and hurt were broken. Little by little, the chains loosened and I saw things clearly. Slowly I began the process of healing and reconciliation with my God. "Come here. I've been waiting for you. I knew you'd be back," He said to me.

I get emotional thinking about all this, because it was such a defiant, lonely and angry time. I hope the lessons learned will never dim in my memory.

So here I am, on my own, working two jobs with two children in college, and it's been a struggle. I'd like to say, though, that it's been a triumphant struggle.

Praise God that He is never finished with us. Praise Him also that His love is far better and more perfect than any on earth.

She speaks for so many church members who have drifted away from God. The worst thing about leaving is the feeling that all hope is gone; the best thing about coming back is finding out the Lord is right there waiting for you to return.

A TAILWIND CENTURY RIDE

I share one final story about a man who once attended the church I now pastor, though I never knew him personally. He and his brother were raised in a Christian home and attended church every Sunday. During his college days, he rode his bicycle every weekend from Kalamazoo, Michigan, to Oak Park, Illinois—a distance of 150 miles—so he could attend the college Sunday school class.

Eventually he married, had a wonderful family, and moved to upstate New York. For many years after that he never really had time for God. By his own testimony, even though he attended church regularly he had never made a personal commitment to Jesus Christ.

That began to change one summer when something awful happened. Without warning, he developed a brain tumor. The doctors operated and felt they removed the tumor in time to save his life. That experience caused him to think seriously about his relationship to God. Just before Christmas he got some more bad news. The brain tumor had come back again. This time it was inoperable. The doctors never came out and flatly said, "There's no hope." But that was the message.

The turning point came in the first days of January. He went to see his pastor in New York and said, "I want you to know that even though I have cancer, something wonderful has happened. I have given my life to Jesus Christ." Four days later he started chemotherapy—a desperate attempt to stop the inevitable. That same day he wrote a short note to his brother. With his permission I share part of it with you.

> Brother, thank you and all of your fellowship friends who showed me a good time whenever I came to visit from Kalamazoo years ago. It was witnessing those good people that kept the seed of Christ from dying within me. Now as a result of last fall's health adventure, I have turned to Him. Have witnessed Him, praised and glorified in Him like I never would have imagined. It feels like an all downhill tailwind 100-mile bike ride. Hug everyone for me. Take care of yourself and we will see you for at least a weekend as soon as I am recommissioned to drive, I hope. Love, your maybe bigger little brother.

That weekend never materialized because he died in the wee hours of the morning two weeks later. Before he died, the chemotherapy made him blind. But he could see better blind than he ever saw when he had his sight. That is the grace of God. Another prodigal son had come home.

THE DOOR IS OPEN AND THE LIGHTS ARE ON

I share those two stories with you because you need to know that the story Jesus told still holds true today. *The way back to the Father is always through the far country.* Where is the far country? The far country is anywhere outside the will of God. The far country may be for you like it was for the prodigal son—deep in wild living. But it won't be the same for all of us. The far country is anyplace where your life seems empty and you look up and say, "Is that all there is?" And the Father says, "Of course not. Come home."

If you are in the far country right now, my words to you are very simple: *it's time to come home.* If your foolish decisions have placed you outside God's will, it's time to come home. The door is open, and the lights are on. Take the first step, and the Father will run to meet you.

QUESTIONS FOR PERSONAL/GROUP STUDY

1. When you hear the phrase "out of God's will," what does it mean to you?

2. Read Luke 15:11-32 slowly and thoughtfully. Put yourself in the prodigal son's place. What made him want to leave home? Have you ever felt that way yourself?

3. What made the prodigal son finally decide to come home? How do you think he felt as he prepared to meet his father?

4. Now put yourself in the father's place. Think about the range of emotions he must have felt when his son asked for his share of the estate. How would you have responded in that situation? How did he feel during the long months or years his son was in the "far country"? Why didn't he punish his son when he finally came home? Would you have been tougher than he was?

5. Now put yourself in the older son's shoes. Why is he angry? Have you ever felt like he did? Why? What did the son really want his father to do? What kind of "far country" was the older son in?

6. What does this story teach us about God, about human nature, about forgiveness, about unforgiveness?

GOING DEEPER

For a long time Alex has refused to go to church because years ago he had an affair. Through the help of many friends, he faced his sin, confessed it, and through much hard work saved his marriage. Not everyone at church knows about the affair, but many do, and some can't seem to forgive him. Or at least that's the way Alex feels every time he goes to church. So now he doesn't go at all. When anyone brings up the subject, he gets extremely angry and defensive. As a result, his walk with Christ is stuck in neutral. What could you say to him that might make a difference? And how could you change the atmosphere in your church so that Alex could truly experience forgiveness?

CHAPTER ELEVEN

Dreams, Visions, and Supernatural Signs

I know a Christian man who fell deeply in love with a young lady he met when she came to his country on a short-term missions trip. After a few days together, he truly thought that God wanted them to get married. When she returned to America, he wrote her saying that he knew it was God's will because one day he looked up in the sky and saw a white bird and a black bird flying together. In the same letter he also said that while walking by a stream, he saw two fish swimming together. As he watched, they seemed to kiss each other. What greater evidence could he ask for? Surely this was a sign from God!

Whenever dreams, visions, and supernatural signs are discussed, three questions immediately come to mind. Number 1: are such things really possible today? Number 2: if they are, what part do they have in determining God's will for your life? Number 3: if you think you have had a dream, a vision, or some kind of supernatural experience, what guidelines should you follow in evaluating that experience?

It's certainly easy to go to extremes in this whole area. Some people argue that dreams, visions, and supernatural signs from God simply cannot and will not happen today. If you move to the other end of the spectrum, others believe that such things should be a normal and regular part of the Christian life. And between

173

those two views you can find evangelicals at virtually every possible point along the spectrum, from "It might happen, but I doubt it" to "It could happen occasionally" to "God often communicates this way" to "You should expect signs and wonders in your life" to "You should seek supernatural signs" to "Signs and wonders are for all Christians all the time."

With this in mind, I want to suggest that the truth lies somewhere between the extremes of never and always.

WISHING FOR A MIRACLE

One point I have stressed over and over again in this book is that *discovering God's will is a step by step process.* Trying to discover what God wants you to do is not something you do early in the morning while you are getting dressed. It's a process. After all, most of life's decisions are very difficult. Some of them are extremely complex. Often we come to the moment of decision and truly don't know what to do. It is at those moments that we wish God would speak directly to us.

We dream of going upstairs in the morning to the second-floor window, looking outside, and finding a message from God written in four-foot-tall letters in the grass below: "Go to China and be a missionary." "Sell your house and move to Vermont." "Enroll in medical school." "Don't worry about your grandmother. She's going to be fine." "Don't marry Frank. Marry Ed instead."

Some Christians claim to have experiences of that nature on a fairly regular basis. They leave the impression that whenever they come to a point of decision God somehow miraculously speaks to them.

Our problem is that for every person who fits into that category there are many others who go for years and even for a lifetime and never have anything mystical or seemingly supernatural happen at all.

It is possible for those who find themselves in that second category to begin to feel like second-class citizens. If you listen to the people in that first group very long, you may begin to wonder, "Is something wrong with me? Am I not praying enough? Am I not godly enough?"

I regard myself as being in this second category. Although there have been a few occasions when it seemed that God was speaking supernaturally to me, those moments have been few and far between. My conclusions in this chapter come in part from my personal experience and in part from many conversations with Christians who are confused about dreams, visions, and supernatural signs. The biblical material comes from several years of study and theological reflection, from which I have discerned five basic truths.

TRUTH #1:
In Bible times God often revealed His will through supernatural means

The key word is "often." *There are many examples of God speaking supernaturally at certain points in biblical history.* For instance, the Bible records God's conversation with Adam and Eve, His instructions to Noah to build an ark, His call to Abraham in Ur of the Chaldees, the story of Moses and the burning bush, Jacob's ladder, Joseph's dream, Gideon's fleece, Samuel hearing the voice of the Lord, Daniel's vision of the four creatures, the handwriting on the wall, Joseph being warned in a dream to take the baby Jesus to Egypt, Peter's vision of the animals being lowered out of heaven, Paul's encounter with Jesus on the Damascus Road, and Paul's vision of the man from Macedonia. In this category we ought also to put John's vision on the Isle of Patmos, which makes up most of the Book of Revelation. Even a casual reading of the Bible confirms that God often communicated using supernatural means.

TRUTH #2:
God did not communicate this way all the time, nor did He do it for all the people in the Bible

Some commentators have observed that many of the supernatural events occurred during three crucial time periods: Moses and the exodus from Egypt, the days of Elijah and Elisha, and the life of Christ and the first few years of the Christian church.

To make that observation is not to deny that God revealed Himself supernaturally to the patriarchs and through the prophets of Israel.

But clearly there were periods of time in the Old Testament when no unusual, miraculous manifestations took place. Abraham evidently didn't hear directly from God every day; neither did Jacob or Elijah or Daniel. As far as we know, the average Israelite in Beersheba or the average Christian living in Cappadocia may have lived his entire life without ever experiencing any supernatural revelation from God.

TRUTH #3:
God spoke supernaturally at
critical moments of history

He spoke to Abraham when He called him to leave Ur of the Chaldees. He spoke to Joseph when He wanted to reveal His plan for the nation of Israel. He spoke to Moses when He called him to lead His people out of Egypt. In Acts 10 He gave Peter the vision of the clean and unclean animals being lowered together out of heaven when He wanted Peter to understand that the Gospel was not just for the Jews but also for the Gentiles. In Acts 16 He spoke to Paul supernaturally when He wanted Paul to understand that he wasn't to stay in Asia Minor but was to move west into Greece and eventually on to Rome.

If you begin to look at these events, one pattern emerges: *God used supernatural means to communicate His will at critical moments of history*. Abraham had to leave Ur so God could raise up the nation of Israel. Moses needed to lead the children of Israel from Egypt to Canaan. Peter had to learn that the Gospel is not for Jews only, but for Gentiles as well. Paul had to discover that God had chosen him to take the Gospel to Europe.

This point, if not pressed too far, may be useful in helping us think about various supernatural signs that may happen today. I can find no particular biblical objection to the notion that at some critical juncture in your life God *might* (here I speak with due caution) use some unusual event to confirm His will to you. Such things did happen occasionally in the Bible, though not every day and not to every person. Therefore, it doesn't seem wise to rule them out completely today.

TRUTH #4:
There are some dangers associated with focusing on dreams and visions and the supernatural

I think there are at least three dangers in focusing on supernatural events in your Christian life. First, there is the danger of elevating the unusual over the ordinary. Second, there is the danger of elevating your personal experience over the Word of God. Third, there is a very real possibility that you will actually miss God's guidance because you are focusing on the spectacular and on the unusual when God might be revealing His plan for you through the ordinary circumstances of life.

TRUTH #5:
God may use supernatural means to lead His people today

We know that He did so in biblical times. We also know that His power is the same today as then. However, that does not prove that at any given moment God will speak supernaturally today. I'm not sure how one would prove that in a particular circumstance, at a given place and time, God is revealing Himself supernaturally.

For instance, I do not doubt that God can directly and miraculously heal the sick according to His will. Almost every pastor has prayed for someone desperately ill and has seen them make a miraculous recovery. If that happens sometimes, why doesn't it happen all the time? Instead of blaming the sick for not having enough faith or the pastor for not being spiritual enough, the real answer, it seems to me, lies in the sovereignty of God. There are mysteries here that the human mind cannot fathom. Yet we are commanded to pray in faith, and so we do, believing that God will answer according to His will, sometimes in astonishing ways.

By the same token, I believe that God could use a dream or a vision to say something to us, His children, today. Although I tend to be cautious in this regard—both by nature and by theological background—it seems unwise to rule out any possibility of supernatural leading for the Christian today.

THE ROOF HANGS OVER THE EDGE

Several times in my own life I have felt God speaking directly to me. I don't mean that I heard an audible voice from God. I simply mean that something happened that I took to be a message from the Lord. Something of that nature happened during a visit to a mission station in Belize. Not surprisingly, it occurred during a period when I was going through a time of intense difficulty in my ministry.

During the morning hours I taught the book of Romans to a group of eager students. Each night I would lie awake listening to the jungle sounds, my heart racing, my mind imagining one dire scenario after another. I tried to pray but found it incredibly difficult. Fear clutched at my heart, strangling my faith, squeezing out my confidence in God.

On Thursday morning I joined the staff prayer meeting. We began by listening quietly to what the Lord was saying to each of us individually. A missionary from New Zealand said that as an engineer the Lord usually spoke to him in visual images, not in specific words. He said that the Lord had told him to meditate on the small cabins where the workers lived. At first that puzzled him, but then he felt the Lord saying, "Look at the roofs on those cabins." The cabins are built with overhanging roofs because of the large amount of rainfall in Belize. Then the Lord said to him, "The cabin represents My people. The roof represents My protection. My people are worried that My protection won't stretch to the edges of their need. But they needn't worry. My protection is so vast, it goes far beyond their needs."

After sharing that, he looked around and said, "I don't know why God gave me that. There must be someone else who needs that message." The moment he said that, the Holy Spirit nudged me and said, "Ray, that was for you." Tears filled my eyes as I realized that God had brought me from Chicago to Belize at exactly the right moment when I needed to hear a message of hope from God.

Does that qualify as a supernatural experience? It does in my mind. I can't prove it in a court of law, but I have no doubt that God spoke directly to me at a moment of great personal need.

ONE NIGHT IN JUNE

I have had similar things happen a few other times in my life, although I don't know that I have had a truly supernatural vision. As I was preparing this chapter, my mind went back to the month after I graduated from high school. Like many other teenagers, I had no clear idea what to do with my life. Many people had urged me to consider going into the ministry, but I leaned toward a career in journalism. Late at night after everybody in our family had gone to bed, I paced back and forth in my bedroom. I was seventeen years old, about to leave home for the first time, thinking about my life, and wondering what God wanted me to do. One night I had a dream in which I was preaching to a great multitude of people. I woke up and felt as if the dream had been sent by God to me. So I said, "All right, Lord, if You want me, I will be a preacher." No lights, no angelic voices, no music playing in the background. But that night changed my life. From that moment until now I have always believed that God called me to be a preacher of the Gospel.

Let me be clear at this point. That dream was not in the same category as Joseph's dream or Peter's vision. It may have been simply the logical result of all the days and weeks of pondering my future. Others may dismiss the whole thing as the product of adolescent imagination. But I can tell you that it actually happened to me. And it was a turning point in my life.

As I write these words, I don't feel any particular need to defend myself. I simply pass along my own experience for your consideration. I have never heard God's voice speaking audibly to me, and I suppose that I would be filled with fear if I did. Nor do I seek such experiences. But why should it be thought strange that God would occasionally use unusual means to communicate encouragement and guidance to His children?

FIVE CRUCIAL BIBLICAL TEXTS

With that as background let's look at five passages that will help us think biblically about this whole subject.

Numbers 12:6-8

> When a prophet of the LORD is among you, I reveal myself to him in visions, I speak to him in dreams. But this is not true of my servant Moses; he is faithful in all my house. With him I speak face to face, clearly and not in riddles.

Notice the contrast in these verses. Prophets receive visions and dreams, but God speaks to Moses "clearly and not in riddles." Don't miss the point: *dreams and visions are inherently ambiguous and difficult to understand.* When you have a dream, how do you know what it means? When you have a vision, you still have to interpret it. A dream or a vision is like a riddle. That's why there is a cottage industry in America that has grown up around dream interpretation. If you dream about a tree, how do you know what it means unless someone tells you? Otherwise, you are just guessing.

Consider the case of a college student praying for guidance about being a foreign missionary. That afternoon he sees a cloud float overhead, and the cloud appears to be in the shape of Japan. So he concludes that God wants him to go to Japan. How do you know it's Japan? How do you know it wasn't Vietnam? Or Argentina? It didn't say Japan. It just looked like Japan. Clouds change shape *every few seconds.* If he had looked two minutes later, he would have gone to Greenland. That's the point in Numbers 12:6-8. Even if you have a dream or a vision or a sign, it's ambiguous in and of itself. You can make it mean almost anything you want it to mean.

Psalm 119:105

"Your word is a lamp to my feet and a light for my path." Without God's Word we are left to our own unreliable devices. But when we let the light of the Bible shine upon our path, we are kept from falling into the ditch of foolish decisions. How often it happens that as we read the Bible on a daily basis, we discover that the passage we read in the morning was just what we needed for the situation we faced in the afternoon. God often fits His Word to the practical need of the moment. So out of the ancient prophecy of Micah or the practical words of Proverbs or the call to faithfulness in Hebrews 10 comes exactly the word from the Lord we needed to hear.

Jeremiah 23:25-29

"I have heard what the prophets say who prophesy lies in my name. They say, 'I had a dream! I had a dream!' How long will this continue in the hearts of these lying prophets, who prophesy the delusions of their own minds? They think the dreams they tell one another will make my people forget my name, just as their fathers forgot my name through Baal worship. Let the prophet who has a dream tell his dream, but let the one who has my word speak it faithfully. For what has straw to do with grain?" declares the Lord. "Is not my word like fire," declares the Lord, "and like a hammer that breaks a rock in pieces?"

This is a very solemn warning from God. False prophets constantly claim to have special messages from God. Like David Koresh of the Branch Davidians, or like Jim Jones of the People's Temple, they set themselves apart as having a direct line of communication with God. One way to spot a false prophet is to ask this simple question: *does he believe that he has a special message from God, given only to him and not to anyone else?* When you hear a person make such a claim, beware. False prophets love to speak about their private communication with the Almighty. As Jeremiah says, they speak visions from "their own minds," spinning grandiose tales that come from their own overheated egos.

The warning is clear: don't trust in dreams, but in the written Word of God.

2 Timothy 3:16-17

"All Scripture is God-breathed and is useful for teaching, rebuking, correcting and training in righteousness, so that the man of God may be thoroughly equipped for every good work." The key word is "God-breathed." God literally breathed out the words of Scripture as He guided the minds of the Bible writers. That means that as Moses wrote the Pentateuch, God supernaturally guided the process so that as Moses wrote his words, he was also at the same time writing the very words God wanted written The same is true for David, Isaiah, Luke, Paul, John, Peter, and all the other writers of Holy Scripture. What they wrote was truly theirs, based on their thought, their study, their insight, and was ultimately expressive of their own personality; yet it was at one and the same time *theopneustos*—God-breathed.

Why is this important? Notice the four purposes for the Word of God in verse 16. It is given to teach us, to rebuke us, to correct us, and to instruct us. Why? So that we may be equipped for everything God has for us to do. To be "thoroughly equipped" carries with it the idea of being fully prepared so that no situation in life can catch you off guard. *There is something in the Bible to fit every case.* Whatever duty you have, whatever predicament you may find yourself in, the Word of God will equip you to face it with confidence.

The meaning is this: *God's Word is sufficient*. Nobody can add anything to it; nobody can take anything away from it. Build your life on the Word of God. Get your roots down in the Word of God. Find out what God has said in His Word, and you will discover His will for your life.

CHECK YOUR VISIONS BY THE BIBLE

Here's a good test for those who think they have a vision from God. Check it out by the Bible. *If it contradicts or conflicts with the Word of God in any way, shape, or form, it is not from God, because God will not contradict Himself.* He has already spoken in His Word. So, check the vision or dream by the Word of God. Is it compatible with the Word of God? Does it reflect the will and Word of Jesus Christ? God's Word is the supreme standard for judging any vision, dream, or unusual circumstance.

1 Thessalonians 5:19-22

"Do not put out the Spirit's fire; do not treat prophecies with contempt. Test everything. Hold on to the good. Avoid every kind of evil." These verses tucked away at the end of 1 Thessalonians are often overlooked, but they are actually quite instructive for our purposes. Here we have a balanced approach to the question of supernatural experiences.

On the positive side, don't put out the Spirit's fire. The Bible often uses the symbol of fire to picture the action of the Holy Spirit. Like a blazing fire, the Holy Spirit warms the heart, enlightens the mind, empowers the spirit, and burns away the dross of carnality. When the fire of the Spirit begins to move in a congregation, the results may be so supernatural that some believers may be tempted to "quench" (KJV) the work of the Spirit.

How might that happen? First, *you might do it by stifling the Spirit's work in your own life*. That happens whenever you say no to God. Perhaps He is calling you to take a step of faith, to follow His divine guidance, to move out of your comfort zone, to exercise your spiritual gifts in a brand-new way, to demonstrate the reality of forgiveness and reconciliation in a broken relationship. Saying no in those situations is like throwing cold water on the fire of the Holy Spirit. Don't be surprised when your life begins to grow cold.

Second, *you might do it by stopping the Spirit's work in someone else's life*. First Corinthians 12 speaks of various manifestations of the Holy Spirit. It speaks of differing operations and differing gifts. This can be a risky concept because we aren't all alike! God made you a unique creation. He gave you a combination of gifts, talents, and abilities that He gave to no one else in all the world. It's all too easy to become harsh and critical toward other believers who don't see things exactly as you do. It's perfectly legitimate to say that the Holy Spirit may work in your life differently than He may work in my life.

But that leads to a second question: are we supposed to accept everything people say and do? The answer, of course, is no. To accept everything is to become naive and gullible. That is why Paul says, "Test everything. Hold on to the good. Avoid every kind of evil" (1 Thessalonians 5:21-22). The word "test" means to examine anything that purports to be from God to see if it is genuine. Hold fast to that which is good—i.e., in accordance with God's standard of truth. Reject everything that either appears to be evil or produces an evil result.

We might paraphrase 1 Thessalonians 5:19-22 in this way: "Be open to the work of the Spirit in the body through various gifted people. Examine everything carefully. Hold on to that which is good and true. Reject everything that is evil or produces evil." To the grumpy, supercritical believer who is closed to the work of the Spirit, God says, "Be open." To the gullible, untaught believer easily swayed by supposed supernaturalism, God says, "Be careful." A balanced approach says, "Let the Spirit move freely in your midst, and let everyone carefully examine the results."

This standard is not hard to apply. Suppose you watch some TV preacher who claims to have a message from God. Test it. What if somebody comes to you and says, "I've got a message from God for you"? Test it. When a friend says, "I had a vision, and this is what I think God wants us to do," test it. That is what the Bible says. Test it. Don't put out the Spirit's fire. Don't despise what the prophets say. Test everything; hold on to the good; reject that which is evil.

A WORD OF CAUTION

Let me share a piece of advice with you. *Do not ever make a major decision in your life solely on the basis of what you believe to be a supernatural experience.* That's almost always a mistake. Don't get married just because you had a vision. Don't go to college just because you had a dream. Don't move to Japan because you saw it floating overhead in the clouds. Don't kiss a young woman just because the fish were kissing each other. You'll get in trouble that way. Don't make a major decision in your life solely on the basis of that which appears to you to be supernatural.

THE FOUR-WAY TEST

Here's a simple four-way test for anything that appears to be a supernatural message from God to you:

The Test of Scripture

Test it by the Word of God. Many foolish decisions would be avoided if we simply applied what God has already said to the situation at hand. For instance, you don't need to pray about marrying an unbeliever because God has already told us His will in this area (2 Corinthians 6:14). Nor do we need to wonder if it is God's will for us to show compassion to the poor. You only need to read Proverbs 19:17 and 21:13. How should we respond to those who hurt us deliberately? Ponder the words of Jesus in Luke 6:27-31. What if you think God wants you to commit suicide? Before you pull the trigger, read Exodus 20:13, Deuteronomy 30:19, and John 10:10. Sometimes we struggle to discover what we call "God's will" when we forget the Bible is a book filled with God's will. Through commands, precepts, proverbs, and abundant examples, it teaches us what the will of God is. Are you tempted to ingratitude? Read 1 Thessalonians 5:18. Do you delude yourself that God isn't bothered when you look at pornography? Memorize Matthew 5:28.

This list of examples could be extended almost indefinitely. God's Word speaks to every situation of life. You will never encounter a situation to which the Bible does not speak either in terms of direct command or general precept. That's the first test for any supposed supernatural experience: is it consistent with what God has said in His Word?

The Test of Time

Let's suppose you get a supernatural sign of some kind. *Wait before you make a major decision.* Wait a day. Wait a week. Wait a month. If it's from God, it will still be from God next week. If it's from God, it will still be from God a month from now. Don't be afraid to wait for the Lord to send further confirmation.

The Test of Counsel

Proverbs 19:20 offers this wisdom about receiving advice: "Listen to advice and accept instruction, and in the end you will be wise." *As a general rule, God will rarely speak to you in such a way that no one else around you recognizes it as the voice of God.* If it is truly of God, other spiritual men and women normally will recognize it as well.

The Test of Confirmation

If you have a dream or a vision or some other unusual event that seems like a message from God, ask Him to confirm it by non-supernatural means. Ask God to show you biblical principles that line up with your experience. Search the Word for His instruction. Spend time in prayer with others. Seek godly counsel. Wait on the

Lord. Spend a day fasting before the Lord. Set aside time for extended prayer. Keep a journal of your thoughts and insights. Search for confirming circumstances. If your dream is from God, He will be glad to confirm it for you. Don't make a major decision until you have received that confirmation from other sources.

FIVE PRACTICAL CONCLUSIONS

Let's wrap up this chapter with five practical conclusions. What are we to do about dreams, visions, and supernatural signs? Here are five pieces of advice for you.

Don't Rule Them Out

Although I tend to be very skeptical about many supposed supernatural revelations, I don't think we should go to the opposite extreme and rule them out altogether. Why run the risk of putting out the Spirit's fire? There's a danger that we will become so rigid in our faith that we unconsciously say, "God, You can only speak to us this way. You can't speak to us that way." He's God. He can speak to us any way He desires.

Don't Seek Them

Don't seek supernatural signs. This is where people get in trouble. *They attempt to make commonplace that which is by definition very rare.* Many Christians never have a supernatural experience of any kind. It doesn't matter. You are not a less spiritual Christian if these things don't happen to you. I wouldn't recommend that anyone ask God for a vision or some other supernatural event. If God wants to communicate to you that way, He can do so at any time. By seeking such things you may be opening yourself to false spiritual experiences. And you may be setting yourself up for a fall if God doesn't meet your expectations.

Don't Try to Force God's Hand

Some people try to force God to give them a miracle. They think that by doing certain things they can cause God to respond in certain ways. "Lord, I'm going to fast until You send me a supernatural sign." It's usually a mistake to try something like that. You may end up starving to death. The Bible warns against putting

God to the test; that is, don't attempt to usurp God's rightful place as the Sovereign Lord of the universe.

Stay in Touch with the Holy Spirit

Stay open to the Spirit's working in your life. He wants to guide your life moment by moment. Let Him guide you in any way He sees fit. The Lord rarely leads us in the same way every time. *Above all, make sure you are filled with the Spirit, so He has free reign in your life.* The issue is not supernatural signs, but being so yielded to the Lord that you are fully responsive to the Lord's work in your life.

Build Your Life on the Word of God

Don't make the mistake of building your spiritual life on signs and wonders. God never meant for you to be a "miracle junkie," rushing from one emotional high to another. What will you do when the miracles stop coming? Or your dreams become ordinary? Or the clouds stop looking like Japan? Or the fish stop kissing each other? Or the roof no longer hangs over the edge of the cabin?

There is only one solid foundation for your life—the Word of God.

Can God work miracles today? Yes. Does He? I believe the answer is yes. Might He work a miracle in your life or communicate His will to you in some unusual way? I think the answer is yes to all those things. Certainly God often answers our prayers in ways that are beyond human understanding.

But our greatest need is not for more miracles, but to know the awesome God who reveals Himself to us in the Bible. As we learn more about Him through the Word of God, we will build our lives on a foundation that can never fail.

You may have dreams, visions, and supernatural signs or you may not. It doesn't matter one way or the other. *Build your life upon the Word of God.* When you come to the end, you will not be disappointed but will be delighted to discover that God has kept His word to you.

QUESTIONS FOR PERSONAL/GROUP STUDY

1. Would you like to have a dream or vision or supernatural sign? Would that encourage your faith if you knew it came from God? Why or why not?

2. Have you ever had a dream or vision that seemed to contain some message from God to you? Describe it. What decisions (if any) did you make on the basis of what you felt God said to you? What principles should a person use in evaluating such an experience?

3. Do you believe that if you had more faith you would see more miracles in your life? Why or why not?

4. Do you agree with the statement that "you should never make a major decision solely on the basis of a supposed supernatural sign from God"? What are some potential dangers?

5. What are the dangers of *seeking* messages from God through dreams, visions, and supernatural signs?

6. Why is it important that we build our lives upon God's Word? Name three or four good ways to do that.

GOING DEEPER

Since this chapter touches on an area about which Christians sometimes disagree, it's possible that you would prefer to state things differently. As a useful exercise, go back through this chapter noting areas of agreement, disagreement, and areas about which you have questions or need further clarification. Then write a one-paragraph statement of your understanding of the role of dreams, visions, and supernatural signs in discovering God's will. When you are finished, show it to a friend and ask for some feedback.

CHAPTER TWELVE

How to Make a Tough Decision

> Trust in the LORD with all your heart and lean not on your own understanding; in all your ways acknowledge him, and he will make your paths straight (Proverbs 3:5-6).

T hese two verses are among the most beloved in all the Bible. You may have memorized them in Sunday school when you were a child. Or perhaps you made a cross-stitch pattern of these words and hung it on your wall. Or you may have learned to sing these words as part of a contemporary worship chorus.

G. Campbell Morgan said that when he was leaving home for the first time, his father pressed a note into his hand. When Campbell Morgan unfolded it, he discovered it contained just one verse of Scripture: "In all thy ways acknowledge him, and he shall direct thy paths." Looking back years later, he noted that his father had written that verse with no accompanying comment. No comment, he said, except the comment of his father's godly life.

This text is striking in its simplicity. There is nothing difficult about it. It is so simple that it can be understood by the youngest believer, and yet it is a comfort to the oldest saint of God. And it is good for everyone in between.

These words cling to the soul because they speak to a great

need we all feel—the need for guidance. Proverbs 3:5-6 suggests the basis on which guidance will come. *It is a short course in knowing God's will for your life.* If you learn what this passage is teaching and begin to apply it to your daily life, it will make a profound difference when you need to make a tough decision.

I am beginning this chapter with the assumption that some of us have known these verses for a long time. Sometimes when we know a passage so well, we almost know it too well. We have heard it so often that we have never stopped to think about what it is really saying. Familiarity can breed contempt. You may even be thinking, "I already know this verse—maybe I'll skip to the last chapter." Please don't do that. I want you to capture the truth of Proverbs 3:5-6 in a fresh way.

FIVE KEY WORDS

Not long ago I had a chance to study these verses in depth for the first time. As I did, I discovered that five key words unlock the message of this text. Let's take those key words one by one and see what each one teaches us.

Trust

"*Trust* in the LORD with all your heart." The word "trust" in Hebrew means "to lean with the full body," "to lay upon," "to rest the full weight upon." In our thinking the word *trust* means to rely upon or to have confidence in. But the Hebrew word is stronger. It is the idea of stretching yourself out upon a bed or resting on a hard surface. The word means to put your full weight on something. *To trust in the Lord is to rest your whole weight upon him*—to depend on Him completely.

Lean

"*Lean* not on your own understanding." To "lean" means to rest upon something for partial support. Leaning is what you do when you walk with a cane or hold on to a walker because you are unsteady. This word is used for leaning against a tree or a stone cliff. You lean on something when you are not strong enough to stand alone.

Understanding

"Lean not on your own *understanding*." "Understanding" refers to the mental processes by which you analyze a problem, break it down into its smaller parts, and then make a decision about what you are going to do. Early in the morning when you make a list of all the things you have to do that day, you use your understanding to sort out your priorities. Or it's what you use on Sunday night when you map out the upcoming week. That's understanding. You use it any time you plan your life or solve a problem. Understanding is the decision-making ability that God has given you.

When you take the word "lean" and bring in the idea of "understanding," then add the negative, the meaning is something like this: "use all your mental powers, but do not lean on them for total support." Don't trust in your own ability to figure out your life. Lean instead on the Lord! Rest your weight on Him!

Acknowledge

"In all your ways *acknowledge* him." I am going to stop and say a little bit more about this word because I think "acknowledge" doesn't do full justice to the original text. In the Hebrew this word is an imperative—a command. You could translate this by saying, "In all your ways *know* him."

The Hebrew word means to know deeply and *intimately*. It's the kind of knowing that comes with personal experience. It means to know something through and through.

For instance, somebody might say, "Do you know the President of the United States?" I would say, "Sure, I know the President." If the President walked in the room, I would know who he is. If I heard his voice coming over the TV, I would recognize it. Or if I saw his picture on the front page of the newspaper, I would know it was the President.

Now, I don't really *know* him. I can't pick up the phone and call the White House and say, "Mr. President, this is Ray Pritchard. Let's do lunch this week." He won't take my call because I don't know him personally. I just know him at the level of head knowledge. I don't know him intimately or on a friendship level.

There is another kind of knowing. My wife and I know each other in a completely different way. We've known each other intimately for over twenty years. After being together that long, strange things begin to happen. I will be sitting in the car thinking about a song.—and she'll start singing it. How does that happen? I don't know. Or I will be thinking about a question, and before I can ask it, she'll blurt out the answer. How does she do that? I don't know. Or I'll start a sentence, and to my great consternation she will finish the sentence before I do. When I say, "How can you do that?" she says with a smile, "I know what you are thinking even before you say it."

Things like that happen to all married couples eventually. When you live together that long, you get to know each other at such a deep level that you actually begin to know what the other person is thinking even as he or she is thinking it. You know what your wife is going to say before she says it. You know what your husband is going to do before he does it. You have a deep, personal, intimate knowledge of each other.

Seen in that light, we might translate verse 5 this way: "In all your ways know God intimately . . . deeply . . . personally. When you know God that way in every area of your life, He will direct your paths."

Direct

"He will *make your paths straight.*" That brings me to the fifth word, which in the *King James Version* is translated, "He shall direct your paths." That isn't bad. But I think the NIV translation is a little better: "he will make your paths straight."

This has the idea of a road that appears to be impassable. The road winds through the mountains and down into the swamps. It seems to have a thousand switchbacks. As you study it, you discover that portions of the road are washed out, others are filled with potholes, and still others are blocked by huge boulders. In some places the road apparently becomes a dead-end.

This is the road of your life. As you look at it, it appears to be covered with boulders and rocks. Some parts of it seem to be filled with potholes; other sections appear to be going nowhere. That's the way life is.

But here is God's message to you from Proverbs 3:5-6: *if you will know God in every area of your life, He will take personal respon-sibility to make your way smooth and straight.* He will remove the obstacles if they need to be removed. He will fill in the potholes if they need to be filled. He will redirect the detour so that what seemed to be a dead-end turns out to be the shortest way to reach your destination.

All you have to do is trust in the Lord. Lay yourself com-pletely on Him for full support. Don't lean for support on your own human understanding. In all your ways know God inti-mately. He will take the path of your life that seems to go up and down and around and sometimes seems to curve backwards, and He will make your way straight. That's the promise of Almighty God to you.

TOM'S STORY

Tom and Kyle Renard met during college days at SMU, fell in love, and married before beginning medical school in Dallas.

During their training Tom and Kyle felt drawn in different directions, Tom toward surgery and Kyle toward pediatrics. After graduating together, they each entered their own residency pro-grams in the Dallas area.

Tom's surgery program would last five years, qualifying him to practice general surgery at any hospital in America. During his fourth year Tom found himself thinking more and more about pediatric surgery.

But there were problems. Pediatric surgery is a highly spe-cialized field. Most medical schools don't offer it as a specialty. Those that do generally have only one opening per year. As Tom said, the odds were against him because "I didn't attend the 'right' medical schools, didn't go through the 'right' residency programs or spend time working in the 'right' labs. There's a track most people follow, a handful of schools most pediatric surgeons attend, and a few key hospitals that offer the top resi-dency programs." Very frankly, he was an outsider trying to break into a very small world.

But deep in his heart Tom believed God had called him to be a pediatric surgeon. "I don't know how I knew, but it was more than just a desire. I can't explain it, but I sensed that this was the way I should go."

"THREE TIMES IS ENOUGH"

It wasn't easy sledding. After medical school came five years of surgical residency. In his fifth year Tom spent $10,000 visiting seventeen hospitals around the country. Afterward he submitted his top ten hospitals to the matching program, hoping that one of them would choose him. But it was not to be. He didn't win one of the coveted twenty-four spots.

What now? Through medical school and the five-year residency Kyle had loyally supported him, raising their two children and managing a part-time pediatrics practice. By this time he was board-certified, ready to begin a lucrative practice anywhere he desired. After failing to make it on his first try, some of his friends urged him to start a practice and make some money.

But above all else, Tom Renard is a Christian who believes in the sovereignty of God. So he decided to spend a year working with a pediatric organ transplant team, hoping to broaden his experience so he could apply again. Twelve months later he spent another $10,000 visiting the programs he hadn't visited previously, along with several others for the second time. When matching time rolled around again, he wrote down his choices, hoping against hope. For the second year in a row he struck out.

That meant spending another frustrating year hoping to try for the third time. During that year he joined a prestigious adult transplant team at a leading hospital in Dallas. One more time he spent the money, made his visits, and presented himself to faculty members who in some cases had come to know and appreciate him. "Don't worry, Tom. You'll match this time."

With a rueful smile, Tom told me that Kyle said, "Honey, three times is enough. We've spent $30,000 trying to get you into one of these programs. If it doesn't happen this time, we're going to have to do something else." He agreed, in part because he too was weary of coming so close but failing year after year.

"It Doesn't Matter Who Comes in Second"

It happened again. No match. No offer. No one wanted him as their first choice. Sure, there were letters saying, "You were our second choice." One school sent a letter of encouragement signed by every member of the department. "But so what? Finishing second is like finishing 34th. When they only pick one person, it doesn't matter who comes in second."

He was now thirty-two and had been going to school nonstop for twenty-six years—through kindergarten, grade school, junior high school, high school, college, medical school, a five-year residency, and two one-year fellowships. It was time to get a "real job."

What do you do when you have followed the path you think God wants you to follow only to discover that you are not quite good enough? Lots of people would have quit long before Tom did. Meanwhile, his two boys (now three) were growing up all around him, being raised mostly by Kyle.

Add to that the humiliation of being turned down three years in a row because you don't have quite the right pedigree to break into the field of your choice. What do you do then?

The End of the Dream

Tom gave up the dream of being a pediatric surgeon. He had done all any man could do. It clearly was not meant to be. No one could fault him for trying so hard for so long. As he and Kyle prayed about it, they felt that God had closed the door on their dream.

"We gave it up. That's all I can say. After all that time and all that money, we simply said, 'Lord, Your will be done.' Show us what You have for us now."

At about that time an offer came to join a top organ transplant team on a full-time basis. Not as a fellow but as a full-fledged member of the team. "It wasn't what we wanted, but it truly was a generous offer. I could spend two years there and then be fully qualified to head my own transplant center somewhere in America. So we said yes."

More than once Tom wondered why God had let him go through so much training for no apparent reason. He told his friends, "If God had wanted me to be a pediatric surgeon, I'd be one. He must have something else planned for us."

CHICAGO CALLING

A few months passed, and word came that Tom would be sent to England to study under a world-famous transplant surgeon. Just before he left a call came from a doctor at a hospital in Chicago. "We're starting a pediatric surgery program in three months, and we'd like to throw your name into the hopper along with nine others for consideration."

Tom was amazed. He prayed, "But, Lord, we gave up that dream months ago. Why are You bringing this now—just before my trip to England? What's going on, Lord?"

A few weeks later Tom received a call while he was in England. It was the doctor from Chicago with the good news that Tom had been chosen as the first fellow in a brand-new pediatric surgery program.

After all that money and all those interviews. After trying and failing three times. After trying to explain to his friends why he kept applying year after year. After finally giving up the dream. After starting a new life.

After all that, he was finally accepted by a program that didn't even exist when he'd started the process. Accepted by doctors he had never met. He would be the first man in a program for which he'd never interviewed.

What does it all mean to Tom? "As I look back on what I went through, I see God's hand at work at every point of the way. I think of Proverbs 16:9, which says, 'In his heart a man plans his course, but the Lord determines his steps.' God knew all along where He wanted us to go. But we had to give up our dreams in order for us to see God's will completely fulfilled."

Is it a miracle? Tom thinks so. It's not in the same category as turning water into wine, but if you ask Tom, he can see God's fingerprints everywhere he looks.

The turning point came when he and Kyle together laid their dream before the Lord and said, "Whatever You want for us, we're ready to do."

As I write these words, Tom is just finishing up his pediatric surgery fellowship. What's next? He's not sure, but he's excited to see what God has in store.

That's why the search for God's will is so exhilarating. When God is leading the way, every obstacle will eventually be removed. The path may have many twists and turns, but in the end He will make your path straight. You have His word on it.

"BLESS IT ALL, LORD"

So many people struggle at this very point. The Bible says, in all your ways know God intimately, know Him deeply, know Him personally. As a man knows a woman—know God that way. Know Him to that depth. Know Him with that kind of intimacy.

So often we skip this. When we get up in the morning, we say, "O God, help me. I'm busy today. I've got so much to do. Lord, I don't even have time to pray—so here's my list. Bless it all, Lord. I've got to go." We throw our list up toward heaven while we run out the door. What we are saying is, "God, here's my schedule. Please rubber-stamp it with your blessing." And we wonder why our days are filled with frustration.

Many of us go through life leaning almost completely on our own understanding. We like to be in control. I number myself among that group. I like to know what's going on. I like to be in charge of my own destiny. This passage is a warning to all of us who lay out life the way we want it and then say, "Here, God, stamp it with Your blessing because I am going to go out and do it for You."

God says, "I don't work that way. Know Me first. Put Me first in everything, including all your plans, all your thinking, and all your scheming. Put Me first. And I then will make your way straight."

WE WANT A FORMULA—GOD WANTS
A RELATIONSHIP

Do you want to know the secret of knowing the will of God? Here it is: *in everything you do, know God*. But we all want a formula. "I don't like that. Give me a formula. Give me three steps." Proverbs 3:5-6 tells us that the secret is a *relationship* with God.

Let's talk about Joe, who has been dating Shirley for nine

months. When he picks her up for their Friday night date, she asks the logical question: "Where are we going tonight?" "I don't know. I want to take you someplace you like. I wish you would give me a three-step formula so I could know where you really want to go on Friday nights." How would Shirley feel? Angry, upset, frustrated. "How is it that we've been dating every week for nine months and you don't know what I like and don't like? Where have you been all this time?" She has a right to be angry.

We want to reduce our relationship with God to a formula. God says, "Know Me. Spend time with Me. Put Me first in every area of your life because when you do that I will take care of all those details." Wow! This is a revolutionary way of looking at life.

MINNESOTA OR SOUTH CAROLINA?

We're hung up on the decisions of life. Should I go here? Should I go there? Should I live in Minnesota? Should I live in South Carolina? Should I marry Jane or Sue or Ellen or Sherry? Should I take the job, or should I say no?

Here is the teaching of this passage stated in one sentence: *God is much less concerned with what you do than with what kind of person you are.* So when you say, "Lord, should I go to Minnesota or should I go to South Carolina?" you are asking the wrong question. The question is not where are you going to go, but what kind of person you are going to be *wherever you go.* The question is not, who should I marry, but what kind of person am I going to be no matter whom I marry?

WASTING ENERGY ON THE WRONG QUESTIONS

While you are wrestling with the question of relocation, God wants to know, "Are you going to be My man or My woman whether you go to Minnesota or South Carolina or whether you stay in Santa Fe?" If you decide to put God first in everything, it doesn't matter where you live. And if you are not going to put God first in everything, it doesn't matter where you live either.

We focus all our energy on decisions. But God says, "Know Me and I will take care of the details." We want specific direction. God says, "In all your ways know Me, and everything else will fall into place."

WHAT DIFFERENCE WILL IT MAKE IN 10,000 YEARS?

A few years ago I heard someone say that most of our decisions won't matter at all in 10,000 years. That blew my mind at first. What a liberating way to look at life. The next time you face a tough decision, ask yourself, will it really matter in 10,000 years? Ninety-nine percent of what you worried about this week won't matter three weeks from now, much less 10,000 years from now. In the year 2452 it won't matter whether you lived in Minnesota, Santa Fe, or South Carolina. But what will matter is that you have decided in all your ways to know God. That is what will really matter. All these trivial, piddly details that just soak up so much energy will in that day be seen for what they really are—trivial, piddly details.

In light of this text, what is the will of God for your life? *To know God in everything. To see Him present everywhere and in everything, and to live in total surrender to Him.*

The most important thing is not the decisions you face; the most important thing is your relationship with God. And the closer you get to God, the easier it will be for God to guide you in the way He wants you to go.

"LORD, HERE ARE MY HANDS"

Knowing God means using all your energies for him.

> *Lord, here are my hands.*
> *Lord, here are my lips.*
> *Lord, here are my eyes.*
> *Lord, here are my ears.*
> *Lord, here are my feet.*

Knowing God means taking all that you have and placing it at the disposal of the King of kings and the Lord of lords.

Proverbs 3:5-6 ends with a promise: "He will make your paths straight." God is able to remove the obstacles in front of you. He is able to fill in the potholes and turn a dead-end into a four-lane highway. *God rewards those who show regard for Him by leading them straight to the right end and removing all the obstacles along the way.*

We rarely see this in advance. We mostly see the potholes. The boulders block our view. Many times it seems as if there is no path at all. But He will make a way.

No one can say how He will do it. There are thousands of ways in which God leads His children. He leads us through delays, detours, miracles, the advice of friends, unexpected opportunities, suddenly closed doors, answered prayer, unanswered prayer, inner impressions, and a still, small voice in the night.

You don't see it on this side. On this side you see the problems. But when you know God, He leads you step by step. When the journey is done, you will look back and say, "I don't know how I got from there to here, but I do know this: Jesus led me all the way."

"HOW DID WE GET HERE?"

A friend of ours recently used those very words to describe a harrowing experience that involved a change of jobs, a cross-country move, and a total redirection of her life. As the time drew near, the emotional stress of leaving the familiar for the unknown almost overwhelmed her. I think she would probably say that making this particular move was the single most difficult thing she has ever had to do. All along the way she was torn with inner doubts—wanting to do the right thing, but not sure if she was. When I saw her around a campfire one night there were tears in her eyes. "Are we doing the right thing? I'm not sure." Then two weeks later she took a deep breath and moved to her new home. Just before leaving, she made an interesting comment: "How did we get here? In my heart I believe we're doing the right thing, but looking back I'm not sure how we got from Point A to Point B. Only God could have done it because I never would have done it myself." But she smiled when she said it.

Doing God's will often involves great uncertainty and periods of deep doubt. But if you are willing to do what He wants you to do, He then takes responsibility to reach into the chaos of life and lead you step by step to the place where He wants you to be.

THE FINAL SECRET

Proverbs 3:5-6 is true. Thousands of saints living and dead can testify to that fact. He will lead the way. He will remove the obstacles. You will have a straight path for your journey.

One more thought before I conclude this chapter: what is the most important word in this text? One word: "*he* will make your paths straight." Who is the "he" of Proverbs 3:6? *The "he" is the God of the Bible.* The God of Abraham, Isaac, and Jacob. The God of Moses. The God of Israel. The God and Father of our Lord Jesus Christ. The God who spoke, and a thousand million galaxies sprang into being. The God who has numbered the grains of sand. The God who knows the hairs on your head. The God who sees the sparrow when it falls. The God who holds the universe in his hands. *That God, the almighty, all-powerful, all-knowing, ever-present God of the universe*—He will direct your paths. That's the God who says, "If you will but know Me, I will take care of the details. Trust Me. Rest your full weight on Me. Know Me in everything. And I, the God of the universe, will direct your paths."

If God has said He will lead you, then why are you so fearful? If God has said He will take up your cause, then why are you worried about tomorrow?

> *No evil can baffle if He leads the way.*
> *No enemy can stop you if He leads the way.*
> *No opposition can derail you if He leads the way.*
> *No obstacle can stand forever if He leads the way.*

In all your ways know Him, and He will direct your paths. He has promised, and it is so. It may not be easy. It may not be exactly the way you want to go. It may not be what seems to you the shortest way. But He will direct your paths.

All He says is, "Know Me. Know Me deeply and intimately in every area of your life, and I will take care of all the rest."

He promised—and He will not fail; He will direct your paths. You can count on it.

QUESTIONS FOR PERSONAL/GROUP STUDY

1. Proverbs 3:5 says, "Lean not on your own understanding." Yet God gave you a mind, that you might use it wisely. How can we use the understanding God has given us without "leaning" on it for total support?

2. Everyone trusts in something. What are the distinguishing marks of a person who is truly trusting in the Lord? How can you pick such a person out of a crowd?

3. Do you agree that discovering God's will often involves periods of confusion and personal chaos?

4. How do you feel about the statement that "God is more interested in *who* you are than in *where* you are"? Does that mean it's wrong to seek guidance about where you live? Whenever you face a big decision, what priority should be even bigger than making the right choice?

5. Take a look at your own life. What are you doing right now to know God intimately?

6. Do you feel confident about your own future? Why or why not? As you think about that question, where does God enter the picture?

GOING DEEPER

Many Christians struggle with the concept of trusting God *completely*. What is the biggest fear in your life right now? What's the one thing in your life that you're afraid to let go of? Your health? Your spouse? Your dreams for the future? Your job? Your children? Your hopes of one day getting married? Whatever it is, write it on a 3 x 5 card and jot down at the top: Proverbs 3:5-6. Put the card where you can see it every time you open your Bible. Bring your fear before the Lord every day until you can say, "Lord, I'm not holding anything back from You."

CHAPTER THIRTEEN

The Most Important Ingredient

W hen was the last time you played with children's modeling clay? It may have been a while unless you have a house full of preschoolers. As all parents know, children love modeling clay because they can make almost anything with it. When it first comes out of the can, the clay feels cold and clammy and mushy. It's bendable and easily made into any one of a 1,001 different shapes. You can take modeling clay and make a little baseball with it. Or you can make it flat like a pie crust. If you like, you can roll it up and make a baseball bat. Or you can take that thing that looks like a bat and bend it into the shape of a little horse. Then you can turn the horse into a rabbit or a pig, depending on how fat you make it. You can do anything you like when the modeling clay is soft.

WANTED: BENDABLE BELIEVERS

But what happens to the modeling clay when you leave it out for three days? It dries up and becomes hard and brittle. When you try to shape it, you can't because it's not soft any longer.

There are many Christians who are like that before the Lord. They are hard, brittle, and unbendable. They are set in their ways, with their own plans, their own agendas, their own desires.

Christians like that wonder why guidance is hard to find. But it's really not hard to understand. When your life becomes hard and brittle before the Lord, God speaks, but you don't hear. He leads, but you don't follow. He opens doors, but you refuse to enter. That is why there is no principle more important than the principle of being able to be guided, being soft and bendable in the hands of God so He can shape you the way He wants.

We find many examples of this in the Bible:

Samuel said, "Speak, for your servant is listening" (1 Samuel 3:10).

David said, "Teach me your way, O Lord" (Psalm 27:11).

Solomon said, "In all your ways acknowledge him" (Proverbs 3:6).

Isaiah said, "Here am I. Send me!" (Isaiah 6:8).

Saul (Paul) said, "What shall I do, Lord?" (Acts 22:10).

All that I have written so far can be wrapped up in one sentence: *guidable people always receive guidance from God*. Why is that? Because God always speaks loud enough for a willing ear to hear. Therefore, there is nothing more important than being open to receive guidance from God.

How will you find the guidance you need? In one sense, that's a tough question because God speaks to us in a variety of ways. We may hear a sermon, read a passage of Scripture, receive advice from our friends, feel some inner sense of direction, or have doors of opportunity open or close.

A MOST UNLIKELY TEXT

There is a marvelous passage in Acts 16 that pictures for us some of the major ways in which God guides His children. Acts 16:6-10 is the story of Paul and Silas and Timothy at the beginning of the second missionary journey. They had joined forces to visit the churches, preach the Word, and strengthen the saints. As we shall see, their travel plans changed several times. Luke paints the picture in these five insightful verses:

> Paul and his companions traveled throughout the region of Phrygia and Galatia, having been kept by the Holy Spirit from preaching the word in the province of Asia. When they came to the border of Mysia, they tried to enter Bithynia, but the Spirit of Jesus would not

allow them to. So they passed by Mysia and went down to Troas. During the night Paul had a vision of a man of Macedonia standing and begging him, "Come over to Macedonia and help us." After Paul had seen the vision, we got ready at once to leave for Macedonia, concluding thàt God had called us to preach the gospel to them.

You could read this text 150 times and you might say, "I don't see anything in there about discovering the will of God." Yet this little slice of life from the first century shows us how God's will may be discovered in the ordinary affairs of life. What happened to them often happens to us. So then, how does guidance come? Our text reveals four answers to that question.

ANSWER #1:
Guidance comes through obedience in the ordinary

Verse 6 tells us that "Paul and his companions traveled throughout the region of Phrygia and Galatia, having been kept by the Holy Spirit from preaching the word in the province of Asia." *Paul was on a mission from God to preach the gospel.* That's the one motivating factor that explains his life. That's why he made one hazardous journey after another. He determined to go wherever he could to spread the good news about Jesus Christ. The only thing that Paul didn't know was exactly where he was going to do it. The guidance he needed concerned *where* to preach, not *whether* to preach. He would continue preaching wherever he found himself.

99 PERCENT OF LIFE

That leads to a profound insight: *99 percent of life is ordinary.* It's just the same old stuff day after day. You get up in the morning, take a shower, put your clothes on, eat breakfast, get the kids ready for school, go to work, hope the kids are OK, come back from work dead-tired, read the paper, watch TV, try to be nice, eat supper, play with the kids, flop into bed dead-tired, then get up the next morning and do it all over again. That's the way life is. It's the same old thing day after day.

Where do you begin in discovering the will of God? *You begin by doing what you already know to be the will of God in your present sit-*

uation. So many of us live for those mountain-peak experiences, those times when the clouds part and God seems so close to us.

GET UP AND DO IT!

Many people wish those spectacular moments would happen every day. Often when we say, "God, show me Your will," what we really mean is, "Lord, give me some feeling, some insight, some spiritual revelation." And God says, "I have already shown you My will. Now, just get up and do it!"

- What is God's will for a student? God's will for a student is to do his/her homework.
- What is God's will for a doctor? Get up and do your rounds early in the morning.
- What is God's will for a pharmacist? Take extra care as you fill those prescriptions.
- What is God's will for a banker? Take care of the money entrusted to you.
- What is God's will for an accountant? Take care of those books, and do the job right.
- What is God's will for a teacher? Do your lesson plans, and come to class ready to teach.
- What is God's will for a salesman? Know your product, make your contacts, and move the merchandise.
- What is God's will for a football coach? Get your team ready to play the big game on Friday night.
- What is God's will for an assembly-line worker? Show up on time, sober, with a good attitude, ready to work.
- What is God's will for a flight attendant? Be on time, and be in uniform, with a smile on your face.

If you are a young mother and want to know what God's will is, it has something to do with dirty diapers. God's will for young mothers is *more* than dirty diapers, but it's not *less* than that. God's will for a secretary is *more* than typing, but it's not *less* than that. God's will for you is more than showing up and doing a job. But it is not less than that.

So many of us want to live only on the mountaintop. That's not where you discover God's will. *You discover God's will in the nitty-gritty of the valley every single day.* The Bible says, "Whatever your hand finds to do, do it with all your might" (Ecclesiastes 9:10). Why should God show you His will for the future if you aren't doing the will of God in the present?

That's all-important. What do preachers do? They preach. And that's what you see in Acts 16—preachers who are willing to preach anytime they get the opportunity. They are just looking for the right open door. Because they are willing to obey what they know to be the will of God, God is therefore free to show them the next step.

This passage reveals a second principle about how guidance comes to us.

ANSWER #2:
Guidance comes through suddenly changing circumstances

Paul and his team wanted to go east into Asia, but the Holy Spirit prevented them. Question: how did the Holy Spirit do that? I have no idea. It could have been the result of various circumstances preventing them. Perhaps the road was washed out, or perhaps there was Jewish opposition so they couldn't get in. The Holy Spirit could have communicated through an inner impression or even a voice from God. A prophet might have delivered the message. No one knows how it happened. But somehow they knew they were not to go west.

So instead they went north toward Bithynia. Why? They intended to preach the Gospel there. They still had the same purpose—to preach the Gospel; only now it was redirected through suddenly changing circumstances. But as they tried to enter Bithynia, "the Spirit of Jesus would not allow them to." Another mystery. The Bible doesn't explain how this happened. But somehow they knew the Spirit of Jesus was saying no. I tend to think that as they were praying they had a strong impression from the Lord or perhaps someone received a prophecy. But that's only speculation. Somehow the Lord made it clear: "don't go to

Bithynia." So they headed west to preach the Gospel and ended up in a place called Troas.

HAS GOD MADE A MISTAKE?

What was going on here? *God was revealing His will through suddenly changing circumstances.* Have you ever had that happen to you? You had your life all planned out. You were going *this* way. You were convinced that God's will was *this* way. Then the phone call came that changed the course of your life. Or the boss called you in and said, "We're downsizing. Your job has been eliminated." Or the letter came that said, "You are an excellent candidate, but unfortunately our incoming class is full." Or you asked her to marry you, knowing it was the will of God, but she hadn't discovered it yet and so said no. A suddenly changing circumstance. Or perhaps the investment you counted on for retirement didn't come through. A suddenly changing circumstance. Or, like Dave Dravecky, you got cancer. When that happens we think something has gone wrong in the universe. God has made a mistake. It wasn't supposed to happen this way.

Proverbs 16:9 is one of the most profound verses in all the Bible: "In his heart a man plans his course, but the LORD determines his steps." You make your plans, but God determines which way you're going to go. Suppose you say, "I'm going to Bithynia because they need the Gospel," and suppose God wants you instead to go west to Troas. So you try to go to Bithynia, and you are turned away at the border. God says, "I'm going to wash out the road that way, and I'm going to lock the door this way." So even though you wanted to go north, there's nothing that way. You've got to go west! That's what happened to Paul.

Please read the next sentence carefully. *What you call circumstances is really the sovereign hand of God in your life.* The circumstances that come into your life, whether good or bad—all of them together have come down to you from the good and gracious hand of God. They are all ultimately for your benefit and for His glory.

How did Paul decide to go north in the first place? When east was cut off, he had to go north. What made him decide to go west at the end? When the north was cut off, that was all that was left;

so he went west and preached the Gospel. That's what I mean by suddenly changing circumstances. *Proverbs 16:9 tells us that it didn't happen by chance.* It never does for the people of God. Who is it that opens the doors? It's God! Who is it that shuts the doors? It's God! Who gives opportunities? It's God! Who takes them away? It's God! He is the one who is in charge. Sometimes His will is seen by nothing more profound than suddenly changing circumstances.

There is a third principle we must consider when seeking guidance from God.

ANSWER #3:
Guidance may come through supernatural events

This happened in Troas. When they got to that seaport town, Paul had a vision of a man from Macedonia standing and begging him, "Come over to Macedonia and help us." Paul was in Troas, which was in Asia; but Macedonia was in Greece—the continent of Europe. In between is the Aegean Sea. What is the significance of the man from Macedonia? *If Paul goes to Macedonia, he's taking the Gospel from one continent to another.* That represents a major, historic expansion for the Christian faith. From the moment Paul stepped on Macedonian soil, Christianity was no longer an "eastern" religion.

I have already said that sometimes God does speak supernaturally through dreams, visions, and supernatural signs. I also said it doesn't happen very often. But God can do it. That's what He did here. It was a vision, but the vision was in line with the Great Commission to take the Gospel to the whole world. *This dream was completely compatible with the Word of God and with Paul's previous experience.*

ANSWER #4:
Guidance comes through wise counsel
joined with common sense

Acts 16:10 reveals the final principle of God's guidance: "After Paul had seen the vision, we got ready at once to leave for Macedonia, concluding that God had called us to preach the gospel to them." The word "concluding" means to discuss the matter with other people, to debate the alternatives, to figure out the best way to go, and then come to a conclusion. It's a word that implies the strategic use of the mind. It's what happens when you put a puzzle together. You put the pieces together to make it all fit. This particular Greek word was used for taking different colored threads and putting them together to make a beautiful pattern.

Paul, Silas, and Timothy talked it over, discussed everything that had happened—where they had come from, where they couldn't go—and talked about the open door and the vision of the man from Macedonia. When they put it all together, they concluded that God wanted them to go to Macedonia. *That's the final way that guidance comes—through wise counsel and simple, plain, ordinary, garden-variety common sense.*

JUST DO IT!

Notice that once they figured out God's will, they immediately did it. "We got ready at once." Once you have determined the will of God, what's the next step? Just do it! Once you've figured it out, don't sit around and talk anymore. Get up and do it!

Why were they so quick to do it? Because God had called them to preach the Gospel. He had told them *what* to do, He had told them *how* to do it, and now He's told them *where* to do it. But that brings us full circle, back to where we started. Back to the ordinary affairs of life. *The reason they went in the first place was because of obedience in the ordinary.* Because they were so committed to doing God's will, they weren't blown away by a vision; they just fit it into the big picture and said, "Okay, that's where we go." And off they went.

When they went to Macedonia, did they know what was going to happen? Did Paul know in advance who was going to be there to meet him or what the outcome of the trip would be? No! When you decide to do the will of God, will you know in advance what the results will be? No! Why? *Because though God shows us His will, He doesn't show us the future.* What does He show us? The next step! How is God's will revealed to us? Step by step by step!

A PASTOR'S PILGRIMAGE

I have had several chances to put my words into practice. Like most pastors, I have moved more than once. I've already related in the first chapter how the letter came from Texas inviting me to become the first pastor of a brand-new church in a Dallas suburb. As I look back on the decision to go to Dallas, I see God's hand clearly at work, partly by nudging me in the right direction through the inner urging of the Holy Spirit, partly through the advice of friends, and very much through the outworking of the ordinary circumstances of life. Nothing dramatic happened; just a slow unveiling of God's will, one step followed by another by another.

The decision to come to Chicago was quite different. In the first place, I was born and raised in the South. Never had I dreamed of moving to the Midwest. But when the time came to make a decision, I found myself torn between a church in Oak Park, Illinois, and another church in Arizona. After praying and seeking godly counsel, I truly didn't know what to do. I wanted to go to Arizona, but my wife wasn't so sure. My friends were divided—one of them telling me that deep down I was an "Arizona kind of guy." I never got to find out what that meant because for various reasons the church in Arizona interviewed me and then decided to look elsewhere. At the time their decision devastated me. I remember writing God a three-page letter expressing my frustration that He would make such an obvious mistake.

"I THINK YOU SHOULD GO TO CHICAGO"

Meanwhile, the church in Oak Park continued to talk with me. During that period of confusion I traveled to Chicago to preach at Calvary for the first time. There was no problem with that because I knew I was not coming to Chicago. So it was just a fun weekend. Or so I thought.

Things went so well that I agreed to return as a candidate—albeit a bit reluctantly. A few days before our trip we got a phone call from a friend who told us, "I think you should go to Chicago."

Still doubting, we traveled to Oak Park for the candidating weekend. The Pulpit Committee put me through twenty-four different meetings, interviews, and services in four days. By Friday night I was tired and not feeling very well. The five of us were jammed into a single hotel room. I just wanted to go home to Texas. It was a combination of things—the schedule, the unending questions, the unfamiliar environment, the enormity of the move, and a feeling of extreme exhaustion. That night I hit bottom. I told my family that under no circumstances were we coming to Oak Park. Wisely, my wife urged me not to make a final decision until the weekend was over.

The next morning I felt a little better, and Sunday was better yet. By the time we flew back to Texas, we both felt that if God wanted us to come, we could do it.

"I SENSED YOU WERE FIGHTING GOD'S CALL"

Three days later the phone rang. It was the same friend who had called us earlier. She told us a strange story. "Last weekend I felt impressed to start praying extra-hard for both of you. The Lord spoke to me, and I sensed that you were fighting His call to Chicago. So I prayed that you wouldn't fight the Lord, but that you would be open to His will." She told Marlene that she felt led to pray that prayer on Friday and Saturday—the very days when we were struggling so much. There was no way she could know what we were going through, but God spoke to her, and she prayed for us at the very moment when we needed it.

I can't tell you what that did for me. That confirmed what we had already felt—that God wanted us at Calvary.

As I write these words, we have just celebrated my fifth anniversary as the pastor of Calvary Memorial Church. These years have been exciting, turbulent, and unpredictable. They have also been the most fruitful years of my ministry.

Looking back, I marvel that God could bring a reluctant Jonah like me to the place of His choice. I did everything I could to go to Arizona, but God had other plans. With very little cooperation from me, the Lord patiently guided me step by step from Dallas to Chicago—a journey I would never have made on my own. For that reason I've never doubted that I am exactly where He wants me to be. As I think about this, I am reminded of the gospel song that includes these lines: "He doesn't make you go against your will, He just makes you willing to go." That's my testimony. At every step of the way He led me—sometimes through inner convictions, often through circumstances, sometimes through the

advice of friends, sometimes through what seemed to be supernatural confirmation. All of it worked together—just as the Lord
promised—to lead me in the path I should follow.

SEVEN CRUCIAL QUESTIONS

That's my story. But every Christian should have a similar story.
What God did for me was not unique. God has promised to guide
His children, and He will do it.

That brings us back to our key text in Acts 16. *Paul was guidable; therefore God guided him.* That's the message of those verses
that seem at first to contain no message at all.

What happened to Paul will happen to you if you are guidable.
I want to close this chapter—and this entire book—with seven
questions you ought to ask yourself whenever you are facing a
major decision in your life.

1. *Am I in a place of complete guidability?* Are you open to whatever the Lord wants? Or are you so set in your ways that what
you're really saying is, "Lord, guide me as long as You tell me to
go where I want to go"? Are you willing to do whatever the Lord
asks you to do?

2. *Have I studied this issue from every possible angle?* Use your
mind. Write down the pros and cons. Make a list. Take notes.
Research the question thoroughly. Study the decision from every
possible angle. Have you done that?

3. *Have I sought wise counsel?* Many foolish decisions would be
avoided if only we would dare to ask advice from others. Have you
asked for advice from people who owe you nothing but their honest opinion? Have you discussed this decision with people who
have been where you are right now?

4. *Do the circumstances point in one particular direction?* Sometimes
God reveals His will by opening one door and closing another. Is
there an obvious blockade down one road and an open path down
the other? Have your circumstances suddenly changed in some
unexpected fashion?

5. *Have I searched the Scriptures in order to discover what God has to
say about my decision?* This step must not be skipped. I believe that
God's Word will have something to say—directly or indirectly—

about every situation you face. Open your Bible. Read it carefully. Take notes. Underline key passages. Search the Scriptures. Compare one passage with another. Note the commands, the warnings, the many examples. God has something to say to you in His Word. Make sure you give Him a chance to say it.

6. *Is there supernatural guidance I should consider?* This won't always happen. But sometimes there will be circumstances that seem to be supernatural movements of God that you ought to bring into consideration.

7. *Am I willing to do God's will without regard to the consequences?* Remember, the will of God has more to do with *who* you are than with *where* you are. God's will is less a matter of geography and more a matter of the heart. Are you willing to do what God wants and then to leave the consequences with Him? If the answer to this is yes, you are an excellent candidate to know God's will.

FOCUS ON THE LORD—NOT THE DECISION!

I can imagine one objection you might raise at this point. You could state it many different ways, but it goes something like this: "I've been offered a new job and you haven't told me whether I should take it or not!" "I'm in love with two girls. Should I marry Sally or Beth? Or what about Jill over there? You haven't told me what to do!" "I'm thinking about moving to South Carolina or Minnesota, but Oregon is looking pretty good to me. You haven't told me what I should do."

Yes, I have told you what you should do! Your problem is, you're focusing on the decision, not on the Lord. *When we focus properly on the Lord, the decision will take care of itself.* If we believe in God, we must believe that once we are guidable, He will guide us. If we don't believe that, we might as well give up in our search for God's will.

Let me state this in the form of a long proposition: once you are open and soft and bendable before the Lord . . . once you are willing to take the next step . . . once you are willing to do God's will . . . at that point you must believe that when you need to make a decision God will give you whatever wisdom and insight you need *at that moment*, so that whatever decision you make will be His will for your life. You won't have 100 percent certainty, but He will literally guide your thoughts while you are thinking them so that as you are open to Him, He will guide you to exactly the place where He wants you to be!

But what if at that point you make a mistake? I believe that if you are truly open before the Lord, truly soft and bendable before Him, truly guidable, if for some reason you come to the decision and you make a "mistake," He will overrule that decision in the long run and guide you exactly where He wants you to be for your good and His glory. *If God is God, that must be true.*

LIFE IS LIKE A ROLL OF THE DICE

I want to call your attention to two other verses of Scripture. Proverbs 16:33 says, "The lot is cast into the lap, but its every decision is from the LORD." The lot was a method of determining God's will in the Old Testament. I paraphrase that verse this way: "Life is like a roll of the dice, but God is in charge of how the numbers come up." *Because that is true, you can trust Him to give you whatever wisdom you need to make wise decisions and to bring about proper outcomes so that you can do His will every day of your life.*

What's the most important factor? Guidability! "Delight yourself in the Lord and he will give you the desires of your heart" (Psalm 37:4). As you delight yourself in the Lord, His desires are going to become your desires. You are going to be changed on the inside so that the things you really want are the things God wants for you.

Can you discover God's will for your life? Thank God, the answer is yes! How do you discover God's will? You discover God's will today the same way the people of God have always discovered His will: step by step by step.

God has promised to guide you safely on your journey through this life. You can depend on that. He has said He will be your guide even to the end. He has promised, and He cannot fail. Therefore, I will say it for the last time: *if you are truly willing to do God's will, you will do it!*

QUESTIONS FOR PERSONAL/GROUP STUDY

1. In what sense is discovering God's will our responsibility, and in what sense is it God's responsibility to reveal His will to us?

2. What is guidability, and why is it the single most important ingredient in knowing God's will?

3. When you are seeking God's will for the future, why is it important that you do what you know to be God's will right now? What happens when you disregard this principle?

4. How do you feel about the statement, "when we focus on the Lord, the decision will take care of itself"? Is that a statement of strategy or of priority? Does that mean we shouldn't worry about our decisions at all?

5. When you know the will of God, you are to do it. Period. Why it is important not to delay when God's will has become plain to you?

GOING DEEPER

Let's take another look at the seven crucial questions. Think about several recent decisions you have made, or about a major decision you are about to make. Then rate yourself in each area on a scale from 1 to 5, with 1 being "Not true at all" and 5 being "I am very strong in this area."

1. To the best of my knowledge, I am completely   1 2 3 4 5
   guidable.

2. I have studied this decision from every angle.   1 2 3 4 5

3. I have sought wise counsel from many people.   1 2 3 4 5

4. I have taken changing circumstances into   1 2 3 4 5
   account.

5. I have studied the Bible carefully, seeking   1 2 3 4 5
   guidance from God for my situation.

6. I have considered the possibility of supernatural   1 2 3 4 5
   guidance.

7. I am willing to do God's will without regard to   1 2 3 4 5
   the consequences.

Now review your list. Does one area stand out as something that needs more attention right now? Make that area a matter of prayer, asking the Lord to give you specific wisdom for the decisions you must make.